Faith-Guarding Kids In Troubled Times

Faith-Guarding Kids In Troubled Times

by

Charlotte Rahrig

HARRISON HOUSE

TULSA, OKLAHOMA

All scripture is taken from the *King James Version* of the Bible.

Faith-Guarding Kids In Troubled Times

ISBN 0-89274-976-8

Text and Illustrations by Charlotte Rahrig.

Copyright © 1996 by: Charlotte Rahrig
Pastoring Children in the Last Days, Inc.
P.O. Box 700565
Tulsa, Oklahoma 74170-0565

Published by: HARRISON HOUSE, INC.
P.O. Box 35035
Tulsa, Oklahoma 74153

Printed in the United States of America.

LOVINGLY DEDICATED TO:

My Lord and Savior Jesus Christ, the One Who gave me my precious, special, valuable, and important children:

Glori Lee

Gilbert Jeremy

Sally Rebecca

Angelica Lee

Jacob Niles

DEEPEST APPRECIATION TO:

Dianne Paschen, who believes you cannot outgive God, but has made a noble effort trying to. And to Pastor Mark DeBehnke, the tallest man I have ever known.

SPECIAL THANKS TO:

Those who have given their time working on this manuscript getting all the "I's" dotted and the "T's" crossed. They are:

Carol Perry

LeAnna Willis

Harrison House Publishers

Table of Contents

CHAPTER ONE

Discipling Children In Troubled Times

"SINCE THE DAY OF PENTECOST, the Church has been waiting for Jesus to return. My grandpa looked for Him every day. He just *knew* that he was living in the last days. But Grandpa has been gone for years and Jesus still hasn't come!"

Sound familiar?

"Knowing this first, that there shall come in the last days scoffers, walking after their own lusts, And saying, Where is the promise of his coming? for since the fathers fell asleep, all things continue as they were from the beginning of the creation."

II Peter 3:3-4

This chapter goes on to say in verse 8 that *"one day is with the Lord as a thousand years, and a thousand years as one day."* And in verse 9, *"The Lord is not slack concerning his promise, as some men count slackness; but is longsuffering to us-ward, not willing that any should perish, but that all should come to repentance."*

In my own mind, those scriptures settled the question of why Jesus hasn't returned yet. He is longsuffering.

My precious friend Albert was really into Bible prophecy. Albert and his wife, Peggy, had five children. My husband and I still had four of our five children living at home. Two of ours and one of theirs were still in diapers. When Albert and his family came to visit, we had nine little ones among us.

As our spouses gathered the children around the television or to play games, Albert and I would head for the kitchen, where we would spend hours wrangling over the Word.

We used to tease them, calling them heathens while saying we were the spiritual ones. Those were our carnal Christian days of the blind leading the blind. Thank God for His mercy in leading us to truth. I now see the servant's heart of love that was operating through them as they changed diapers and tended little needs so two close friends could fellowship undisturbed around the Word.

Albert would come with his prophecy books, charts and the like, wanting to talk about Bible prophecy. Without being too obvious, I always tried to steer the subject into some more familiar area. Bible prophecy was just too confusing, too complicated for me.

THE TIME-LINE

Years passed. Albert and his family moved to another state. I was home-schooling my children. Then one day, I was reading a giant, seven-foot time-line I had hung on the wall to refer to during our lessons. It covered a tremendous span of time, beginning at the creation of Adam and continuing through all the major civilizations of the world, up to the present day.

The print was very small. I was reading all the different events that had happened — wars, inventions, etc., when suddenly, it all came into focus with the Word. From Adam to 1900 was about a 6 foot, 11 inch span on the time-line. In 1300 B.C., the Babylonians were credited with inventing the simple cart on wheels. From that invention, up until 1900, was the bulk of the time-line. But basically, very little had happened until the turn of the century.

When I was little, I remember my grandmother telling me stories about her childhood, and how she went everywhere in a horse and buggy. Her transportation really wasn't that much different from the simple wheeled cart the Babylonians had invented centuries before. So from the beginning of time up until the turn of the century, it was almost as if knowledge stood still.

As I stood there reading the time-line, it struck me! One of the prophecies of the end time is that knowledge will be increased and many will run to and fro. At the turn of the century, Henry Ford started mass producing the automobile. This was the first

TIME LINE

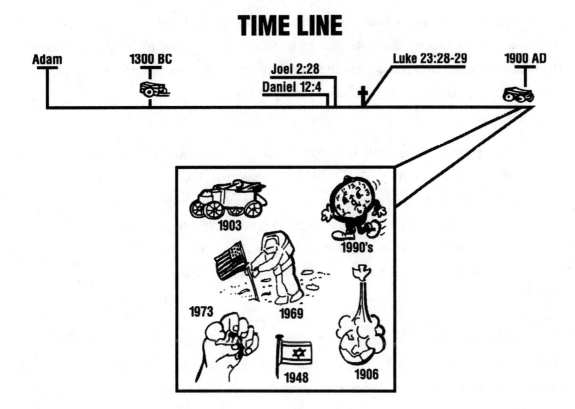

major change from the simple cart and wheel since the beginning of time. On that one little inch on my time-line, civilization had gone from the horse and buggy to the moon and back!

Knowledge is increasing so fast today that textbooks are outdated by the time they are printed. I've heard it claimed that our knowledge is now doubling every year.

The *Baltimore Evening Sun* ran an article by columnist Elsie Chisolm entitled, "Hurry Sickness Victims in Need of Urgent Care." The article dealt with a disease which has reached epidemic proportions among Americans. Pop psychologists call it "Hurry Sickness," manifested by a frenzied life, running to and fro, just as God had prophesied in Daniel 12:4.

As I continued to study the time-line, other prophecies came to mind. Joel prophesied that in the last days God would pour out His Spirit on all flesh (Joel 2:28). In 1906, more than just an increase in knowledge occurred: Azusa Street happened. God poured out His Spirit there and revival swept the world.

On my time-line, a little to the right of center, and roughly 4000 years from Creation, was the Cross. Here, we find Jesus on His way to Calvary, stopping to speak His final prophecy concerning the end times here on earth. The women were following Him, lamenting, so Jesus turned to them and spoke:

"Daughters of Jerusalem, weep not for me, but weep for yourselves, and for your children. For, behold, the days are coming, in which they shall say, Blessed are the barren, and the wombs that never bare, and the paps which never gave suck. Then shall they begin to say to the mountains, Fall on us; and to the hills, Cover us. For if they do these things in a green tree, what shall be done in the dry?"

Luke 23:28-31

How could these women, who in their culture considered barrenness a reproach and shame, even begin to understand a time so wicked that barrenness would be called blessed? Or a time that it would not be good to nestle a little babe to your breast? Yet Jesus spoke of that time, the time of the end, and He said they should weep for the pitiful condition in which they would be. Little did they know what the future held for their children's children. Because there, on that one inch of the time-line, almost to the end of the inch, was Roe vs. Wade and 32 million babies murdered in their own mothers' wombs. Weep indeed.

When I was growing up, there was a family down the street that had twelve children. I can remember when it was bath time each evening before supper. Mrs. Tolliver would call out her front door and all the children came running. No matter what I was doing, picking wild flowers or making mud pies, when I heard her calling, I'd go running along with the others.

She met all her children in the basement where she had a big wash tub on a table filled with warm water. There were wooden steps up one side and down the other. The children lined up at the stairs, each taking their turn in the tub with Mrs. Tolliver washing away the dirt from a long day of play. When they were clean, they would step out of the tub, wrap in a towel and go dress. I was only about three and a half, but I would get at the end of that line and Mrs. Tolliver always let me take a dunk. We had a regular tub in our house, but I thought their basement bath was the neatest thing going.

4

When we moved from Ohio to Florida, our neighbor had eight children. The family was loved and respected in the neighborhood. Their house was always spotlessly clean, with each child rotating chores.

I happened to walk up to the back screen door to knock one day and realized I had arrived at spanking time. On the sofa sat a couple of crying children who had just received their licks. The others were lined up to the left of their daddy, who was seated in a chair with his switch. The mother of the family recited the transgressions of the child about to take his punishment, while the other children waited in trepidation for their own turn to lay across their father's lap.

Quietly, I slipped away. This was one line I wasn't running to join.

The point I'm making here is that large families were once common. Fathers were respected and mothers kept the home. But somewhere along the line, it became fashionable to have only two children, replacing yourself on the planet. Then, it became mother, father, child. Now, you're respected in the eyes of the world for simply remaining husband and wife. Large families are scorned. Yet the Word calls children a blessing.

"Lo, children are an heritage of the Lord: and the fruit of the womb is his reward. As arrows are in the hand of a mighty man; so are children of the youth. Happy is the man that hath his quiver full of them."

Psalm 127:3-5

Adam was told to multiply, and Satan has tried to wipe out man ever since through wars, famines, pestilence and sickness, etc.

The more I looked at that time-line, the clearer the picture became. Prophecy took on a new meaning, as applied to the present. Many prophets say Israel is symbolically the fig tree and the generation that sees the fig tree blossom will also see the return of Jesus. Israel became a nation again in 1948. The fig tree has blossomed. Therefore, according to this interpretation (which I ardently believe), the majority of those alive in 1948 will see the return of Jesus.

5

Is that when His longsuffering will run out? Did God have only five cups of long-suffering? And have we now used 39 ounces of it up? Not so. God the Father has had since the beginning of time an exact time set for His Son to return to the earth. He set that time clock for an exact day and hour that only He knows.

> *"But of that day and hour knoweth no man, no, not the angels of*
> *heaven, but my Father only "*
>
> Matthew 24:36

Because of the Father's longsuffering, the time has been set at a certain point beyond the Cross. And even though we do not know exactly when it will be, as His Church, we are to know the season. In Matthew 24:37, Jesus said that **as it was in the days of Noah, so shall the coming of the Son of Man be.** Didn't God tell righteous Noah to build the ark when He warned him of the flood? It was to the unrighteous that He came as a thief. Sodom was surprised, but God revealed to Abraham what He was about to do. And when the time came, He rescued righteous Lot. Abraham and Lot were not surprised. Only the unrighteous were surprised.

> *"Remember therefore how thou hast received and heard, and hold*
> *fast, and repent. If therefore thou shalt not watch, I will come on thee*
> *as a thief, and thou shalt not know what hour I will come upon thee."*
>
> Revelation 3:3

We will not be caught off guard. We will see the day approaching (Hebrews 10:25). Great men of God in our day sometimes disagree on various subjects, but without question, they do agree on one thing. It is time for Jesus to return. The Church is watching.

> *"Henceforth I call you not servants; for the servant knoweth not what*
> *his lord doeth: but I have called you friends; for all things that I have*
> *heard of my Father I have made known unto you."*
>
> John 15:15

So then, what do these things all mean? We must keep one eye looking up, awaiting His rapidly approaching return; but the other has to be on the lookout on earth, to always be about our Father's business.

Just what is our Father's business in this last hour? Is it the same as it was in the beginning? Yes. He still is not willing that any should perish. So the longsuffering of God is still in place.

THE PERISHING

The important thing in this last hour is to define who is in the most danger of perishing. Where is the attack of the enemy aimed?

"Blessed are thou, Simon Bar-jona: for flesh and blood hath not revealed it unto thee, but my Father which is in heaven. And I say also unto thee, That thou art Peter, and upon this rock I will build my church; and the gates of hell shall not prevail against it. And I will give unto thee the keys of the kingdom of heaven: and whatsoever thou shalt bind on earth shall be bound in heaven: and whatsoever thou shalt loose on earth shall be loosed in heaven."

Matthew 16:17-19

In this passage, Jesus had just asked Peter, "But whom say ye that I am?"

Peter had answered, "Thou art the Christ, the Son of the living God" (verse 16).

Then Jesus told Peter that he was operating in revelation knowledge, and that because of this knowledge, the gates of hell would not prevail against the Church.

Why is this revelation knowledge so important?

Let's take D-Day during World War II as an example. During that maneuver, Germany expected invasion along the northern coast of France. They fortified the coast and concentrated their defenses along the English Channel. But Allied troops landed further west, in an area of Northern France called Normandy. They did so by using the element of surprise to establish a beachhead for unloading more troops and supplies.

It did Germany no good to "bind up" the coastline along the English Channel because that was not where the attack was aimed. But the Germans had no way of knowing that.

Just like the Germans, Satan has been kept by God in the dark. But God has given the Church revelation knowledge. Therefore, the Church *does* have a way of knowing in which direction the attack of the enemy is aimed. Even though Satan throws up smoke screens of scandal in the Body of Christ and stirs up debate over various doctrines, we are able to discern through revelation knowledge the direction of the fiery darts he has launched.

They are aimed at the children.

Because this generation of children will be the last on planet Earth before the return of Jesus, Satan has launched an all-out attack so vicious that it dwarfs the cruelties of the past.

Recent years have brought a new batch of words into our vocabulary: latch-key, values clarification, humanism, gay rights, NOW, and ERA. As a society, we've gone from being shocked over Rhett Butler's comment, "Frankly, Scarlett, I don't give a damn," to open sex and pornography on television. We've gone from prayer in the schools—to abortion counseling—to the distribution of contraceptives in school-based clinics. Parents are working, and children are watching.

The Church is confronted with a whole new set of problems it has never had to face before.

So forget those old simple flannel graphs in teaching the kids of today. These high-tech dynamos will chew you up and spit you out so fast that you will think you've been with Humpty Dumpty in his fall and you'll feel like you can't be put back together again. They burst through the doors of children's church like little ninjas, often disrespectful and spouting adult profanities. Stirred up, hyped up, and not about to shut up, they burst through our doors, and they are perishing.

OUR BLESSED HOPE IN TROUBLED TIMES

STUDY QUESTIONS FOR ADULTS (CHAPTER 1)

There is no fear of the end times for the Christian.

There is much confusion surrounding end-time events. This confusion is often coupled with fear of the unknown. The purpose of this short study is to set your heart at ease. The signs you see occurring should make you rejoice — for your redemption draweth nigh.

Because you are a Christian, you will be saved from the wrath of God that will be poured out in the tribulation times.

Luke 21:36 _____

1 Thess. 5:9 _____

Rev. 3:10 _____

Jesus is coming to meet us in the clouds (Rapture) before the tribulation.

Acts 1:11_____

1 Thess. 4:13-18 _____

1 Thess. 5:1-6,9 _____

2 Thess. 2:1-8 _____

Phil. 3:20,21 _____

1 Thess. 1:9-10 _____

Luke 21:28 _____

We will then spend the next seven years with Jesus in heaven — receiving our rewards...

Romans 14:10 _____

2 Cor. 5:10 _____

1 Cor 3:13-15 _____

and at the Marriage Supper of the Lamb.

Rev. 19:7-9 _____

Jesus then brings us with Him as He returns to the earth, taking vengeance on the wicked and establishing His kingdom.

At the Rapture, we are caught up into the clouds to meet Jesus. In the following scriptures, you will see that Jesus later returns with the saints and His foot splits the mountain. While the scriptures regarding the Rapture are words of comfort, the following verses speak of wrath and vengeance on the wicked. Notice the target of wrath: it is the wicked, not the saints. We will not even get our white robes soiled as Jesus wins the battle with one Word of His mouth!

2 Thess. 1:7-8 _____

Rev. 19:11-21 _____

Jude 14-15 _____

Rev. 1:7 _____

Zech. 14:1-5,9 _____

Zech. 12:10-11 _____

Isaiah 11:4 _____

CHAPTER TWO

Don't Let Your Weapons Weigh You Down

OUR CHILDREN WERE NOW ALL IN ELEMENTARY SCHOOL a few blocks from home. I was enjoying the peaceful, wonderful world of homemaker and mother that I had always dreamed about. I was teaching the Young Married's class at a nearby church, designing quilts for a little mail order business I had ventured into, cartooning for the religious section of our local newspaper, baking, sewing, and painting.

When the children would come home from school, I would proudly display their "A" papers on our refrigerator with little daisy magnets. One day, after getting a glass of juice from the refrigerator, I stood idly gazing at my fifth grader's papers. One, which boasted a bright red 100% at the top, told about the Legend of Atlantis, portraying the legend as a true story. Another paper was on water witchery and dowsing. A third dealt with Greek gods and mythology in a way that made me feel uncomfortable with what my son was being taught.

Those papers, I was to learn, only hinted at a far greater problem.

Calling the school, I made an appointment to look over all my son's curriculum. The following day, after reviewing all the textbooks and other materials, I was disturbed by what I'd read. Deep down, something was terribly wrong, but I couldn't put my finger on it. All I could remember were the comments of a school official who knew me well, who had walked beside me as I left the school and half whispered, "If you think this is bad, go over to the middle school where your son will be next year. Take a look at what *they'll* be teaching him."

Motivated by his comment, I went to the middle school. The counselor there piled a stack of over fifteen books on a table in the school library.

"There they are," she stated briskly. "Let us know when you are finished."

11

She left me alone with the stack. I just sat and began to pray, "Father, I don't even know what I'm looking for. I just feel in my spirit that something is very wrong. Please guide me and show me where to look."

Pulling a world geography book from the middle of the stack and a health book from the bottom, I began to leaf through the pages. I felt like my world caved in that afternoon as I read of the glories of communism and the shortcomings of democracy in the geography book. The health book was even worse! Group masturbation and homosexuality were condoned. Virginity was portrayed as part of the old double standard. It seemed as though every deviate behavior was okay, but nowhere in the book could I find references to the institution of marriage. One page pictured a Bible hanging over a child's head. The picture was captioned, "Choose your values because they really please you, not someone else." With each page I turned came a new wave of nausea.

Finally, unable to take anymore, I notified the school office that I was finished, then drove home and spent the afternoon weeping. I felt like someone who had been walking around with their head in a cloud, unaware of what was going on around them. I felt betrayed.

Now at this point in my life, I still had not learned to handle circumstances as the Word of God directs. The way I handled the situation was to desperately begin to search and find out what was going on in the schools. My husband took over household duties and meal preparation, bless his servant heart. Sixteen days and twenty-seven books later, I came out of my easy chair ready for war.

Newly introduced to the concept of Values Clarification and Humanism, I began to gather evidence to take to the school board. I armed myself with stacks of documents such as a National Education Association publication on Values Clarification stating (contrary to what they claim) that the purpose of values education is to change the student from his values learned at home to those of the school. The publication suggested that we emulate China and Russia, who use this form of education; that the schools should purposely deceive parents to keep from disclosing that these techniques are being used to accomplish their goals.

I took my findings and went before the school board. With me were 350 supporters from area churches and a camera crew from the *700 Club,* who came to film the proceedings.

The school board ignored the evidence and refused to give informed consent to parents. This began a two-year, torturous, all-out battle. A massive letter campaign was initiated. I appeared on numerous television and radio programs, such as Dr. James Kennedy and Marlin Maddoux. I received assistance from Phyllis Schlafly, founder of Eagle Forum, and spent twelve to sixteen hours a day on the phone. Attorneys for People for the American Way had been called in and were carrying on a film propaganda campaign called "Textbooks on Fire," against textbook censors and book banners in my neighborhood school cafeteria.

A call to Eagle Forum confirmed my worst fears. The only thing left to do was sue the school board. They felt that the battle had received so much attention nationally that the NEA and the People for the American Way would feel they had to win the battle. After all, this was the second-largest school district in the nation and very powerful. The combination of monies would be too much for an organization which depended on donations. Eagle Forum attorney John Schlafly said they felt it would be prudent for their organization to support smaller battles in many areas across the country rather than to pour all their resources into one major battle. So there I sat, alone.

The superintendent had exhorted the board members to sue me. The newspaper supported the school board, and they were having a heyday chopping me to pieces. Of course, I was fired from my cartooning job with them. Each day brought a new threat, either by letter or phone. A dead and bloody bird had been left on my doorstep, my mailbox knocked over, my car battery cables were slashed. I was nearly run off the road and my children, who had almost forgotten my name, were being mocked and teased in our neighborhood. My husband had yet to complain, even though we couldn't find our floor through all the literature piled up around my desk and the mess from neglected household duties.

I had used every weapon, tactic and technique I knew of, praying for God to bless it as I went. I was really weighed down with my own weapons, and there I sat, with nothing changed. Two years of all-out war, and the objectionable textbooks were still being used.

The phone rang shortly after I had finished my call to Eagle Forum. It was a producer from "Good Morning, America," inviting me to be a guest on the program. When I hesitated, they even offered to fly my entire family to New York and pay all our expenses. I told them I had to consider their offer and that I'd call them back. I knew if I accepted the invitation that the battle was just going to escalate. Was I ready for more of the same?

Most people probably would have learned their lessons in a few weeks, or at the most, a few months. It took me two long years to come to the end of myself and fall on Him. Laying my head on my arms atop my desk, broken and weeping, I began to sob my dilemma to Father God, having no strength to go on, yet needing to go on. There seemed to be no answer, nowhere to turn. I was so tired, so very tired.

Pretty soon, the sobbing eased. I began to feel a peace wrap around my shoulders and cover me like a warm, protective cloak. Deep within came a stirring and a peace so tangible and so gentle. The following words seemed to float up to my consciousness from deep within:

> *"For though we walk in the flesh, we do not war after the flesh: For the weapons of our warfare are not carnal, but mighty through God to the pulling down of strong holds."*
>
> 2 Corinthians 10:3-4

With that scripture came new strength and understanding. No wonder I was so tired! I had been warring in the flesh, in my own strength, with carnal weapons. Satan was over there in the spirit realm and I was over here in the flesh, striking out. No wonder I did him no harm.

"Finally, my brethren, be strong in the Lord, and in the power of his might. Put on the whole armour of God, that ye may be able to stand against the wiles of the devil. For we wrestle not against flesh and blood, but against principalities, against powers, against the rulers of the darkness of this world, against spiritual wickedness in high places. Wherefore take unto you the whole armour of God, that ye may be able to withstand in the evil day, and having done all, to stand. Stand therefore, having your loins girt about with truth, and having on the breastplate of righteousness; And your feet shod with the preparation of the gospel of peace; Above all, taking the shield of faith, wherewith ye shall be able to quench all the fiery darts of the wicked. And take the helmet of salvation, and the sword of the Spirit, which is the Word of God: Praying always with all prayer and supplication in the Spirit, and watching thereunto with all perseverance and supplication for all saints."

Ephesians 6:10-18

Telling "Good Morning, America" "No," I told God "Yes," and started on one of the most exciting and fulfilling adventures of a lifetime. *I discovered the power of the spoken Word of God and what the Bible taught about spiritual warfare. I learned how to really stand on the promises of God by faith.* After just a short time of standing on God's Word and prayer, the most offensive book was removed from the school system. Using His weapons, I found myself refreshed instead of drained; peaceful, instead of stressful. I saw results instead of getting nowhere. And my family could see the living room floor again!

The enemy has been found. And where is he launching his massive attack?

On the children.

Where does that place those who love, care for, and minister to children?

On the front lines!

CASTING OUR CARE ON JESUS

STUDY QUESTIONS FOR ADULTS (CHAPTER 2)

Is the Christian to worry over the terrible things they see happening in the world today?

Jesus gives us very explicit instructions in the Word of God warning us against worry.

Matthew 6:25-34 _____

1 Peter 5:7 _____

After casting my care on Jesus, do I sit around and just do nothing?

You are a spirit, you have a soul, and you live in a body.

1 Thess. 5:23 _____

It is important to be led of the Spirit of God through your reborn spirit.

Romans 8:14 _____

Two people can be picketing an abortion clinic. One can be anxious and upset, not casting their care on Jesus. They are filled with hatred and strife for the people inside.

James 3:16 _____

The other person is picketing the same clinic, but they have cast the care on Jesus. They are filled with compassion and forgiveness for those inside. They are there because the Spirit of God led them there to help rescue the perishing and care for the dying.

John 15:12 _____

Put on the armor of God, pray in the Spirit, walk in love, and wait on our commander Jesus to instruct you as you cast all your care on Him.

Eph. 6:10-18 _____

John 15:9-10 _____

John 15:5 _____

CHAPTER THREE

The Roots Of Disobedience

BETWEEN seven and eight thousand adults were at the West Palm Beach Auditorium for "Night of Praise." This was my first opportunity to minister to children "big time"! The children were totally mine, just what I had been praying for. With a week of teacher's camp under my belt, and armed with a stage, twenty-six puppets, seven puppet skits, fourteen object lessons, six games, praise tapes, posters and five helpers, I was set to minister to the children.

I faced two hundred little kids — and fell flat on my face.

I had arrived at the auditorium ninety minutes early to get set up, only to learn we couldn't have access to the appointed room until a group of ministers and altar workers concluded their own meeting.

The spirit of confusion took hold even before we began. We attempted to set up with the two hundred children already in the room, wriggling in their seats, scampering around our equipment and peeking at the puppets. The evening was a shambles! At one point, kids ran up and pulled the puppets right off my hands, while my helpers, who would have come to my aid, were chasing down the halls trying to capture rowdy kids who were treating the event like a field day.

Three long hours later, sitting on my boxed-up puppets, I began to think teaching adults might not be so bad, after all. Maybe God was calling me into that area of ministry instead!

Despite my own feelings, the organizers of the "Night of Praise" were pleased with the children's program. They invited me back, not knowing what was going on downstairs. The children seemed to have a good time and didn't interrupt the meeting being conducted upstairs, but I felt like a complete failure.

I now know that there were questions I should have asked the organizers instead of taking certain things for granted. If I had done so, I would have avoided a lot of unnecessary complications.

Something else was wrong, though, and it haunted my every meeting and classroom teaching. After talking to multitudes of other children's workers, I learned that discipline is the biggest problem they faced. Lack of discipline can break your whole program. It can ruin your lessons, burn you out, and make you want to give up children's ministry, because you feel so ineffective. But most importantly, poor discipline neutralizes the truths you attempt to teach the children in the short time you are together.

Using every tool of ministry that I had been taught, and with a heart full of love for the children, I continued to work with the little ones. There were anywhere from twenty-three to forty-four children in the class I taught each week at my little church. Lessons were exciting and inspired. Most of the children enjoyed them and were growing. But each week, I had to deal with a few severe discipline problems. I continued to sense failure. Once, in tears and ready to give up, I turned to the pastor for help.

"Send them back to their parents if they misbehave," he told me.

We tried that, and just about everything else we could think of. We sat them in the hall and stood them in the back of the room. Nothing worked.

The parents were happy because their children were learning while they had the opportunity to worship uninterrupted. But the haunting discipline problem was like a blanket of failure over everything.

Most authorities agree that to be able to teach effectively, the troublemakers either have to be controlled or removed from the room. But I kept remembering a scripture from the Gospel of John.

"While I was with them in the world, I kept them in thy name, those
that thou gavest me I have kept, and none of them is lost, but the son
of perdition; that the scripture might be fulfilled."

John 17:12

Jesus' words to the Father as He completed His mission here on earth showed that He kept every single one God gave Him and none were lost. I couldn't say the same thing. Kids were slipping through the cracks. God gave them to me and I wasn't keeping them.

Now, however, I have total victory in this area, both in that class and in others I've taught since. I haven't had even one problem. I am now able to keep everyone He gives me. There is rarely an interruption in the lessons. No helper is needed, even when I go behind the puppet stage. The children don't utter a word, but sit transfixed and interested.

Sound impossible? It's true.

Once, while traveling in a van with a group of children's workers, each was telling horror stories of discipline problems. I had initiated the conversation, waiting for an opening to share the truths God had taught me. I listened to the frustration and hopelessness in their voices as they related one discipline nightmare after another. How well I knew those feelings. No matter how successful you are, Satan is always ready to remind you of your shortcomings.

Finally, when it was my turn, I talked about how my classes had been and compared them to how they are now, explaining that the difference was based upon a few simple truths from God. There were about ten of us in the van. At my words, all leaned forward in their seats, eager for any word of hope, for any solution. Jokingly, I said, "Okay, I'll pass the hat and each of you drop in $10, then I'll tell you the answer."

They laughed and one said, "Ten, nothing! I'd give $100 or $200 for the answer. Tell us."

DISCOVERING THE ROOTS OF DISOBEDIENCE

Three simple words said it all: "Confession and spiritual warfare." I prefer to call it "warring in the spirit," since so much has been written and said about spiritual warfare that some may simply "tune out." But take heed. This "warring in the spirit" is in a specific area where revelation knowledge has been given.

"And now also the axe is laid unto the root of the trees: therefore every tree which bringeth not forth good fruit is hewn down, and cast into the fire."

Matthew 3:10

My brother, a nurseryman, tends trees and plants by pruning, a process of cutting the branches back. This causes the roots to shoot deeper and the plant to grow back stronger and fuller. This is natural law.

According to the Lord, discipline problems in a classroom are like that tree. The part that we see, the visible part above the ground, is the behavior, the disobedience. But there is a deep, underlying cause for the disobedience. The ax must be laid to the root or the growth will return. There are four main reasons or "roots" for disobedience: Fear, Confusion, Rebellion, and Despair.

In a vision, the Lord showed me a child being prompted by Satan to disobey. The teacher stands the child in the corner and Satan then comes and whispers, "See, even they know you're no good." The teacher was chopping away at a branch, but neglected to put an axe to the roots. The root of despair goes deeper, causing the disobedience to grow even stronger.

Looking up *despair* in the dictionary, I found it describes this generation of children quite adeptly: "Despair — To lose or give up hope; a state of mind caused by circumstances which seem too much to cope with; total loss or abandonment of hope which may be passive or may drive one to furious efforts against adverse circumstances with utter disregard of consequences."

I'm certain any school teacher would describe some of the behaviors they witness as having an utter disregard of consequences. Sadly, in many cases, this carries over into the Church.

During the 1960s, Nikita Khrushchev promised Russia would "bury" the United States. He said they would destroy us from within. Now, almost thirty years later, God is banned from our schools. Drug use, AIDS, abortion and teen suicide are on the rise. Children are taught about all the problems in society but aren't allowed to have the true answer. Each day, they pick up the mirror of the world and look at themselves. What they see is just another animal, wandering aimlessly on the planet, having no specific purpose for their existence. No wonder fear, confusion, despair and rebellion take control of the hearts of children!

Remember, these roots are under the ground, unseen, spiritual. And that should give us hope, because our mighty weapons are in the spiritual realm! As long as Satan can keep us battling in the flesh against what we see, we can't touch him. He wages a spiritual battle. To overcome, we too, must battle in the spiritual world.

"For though we walk in the flesh [children throwing spitballs at us], we do not war after the flesh ["Okay, go stand in the corner"]: (For the weapons of our warfare are not carnal, but mighty through God to the pulling down of strong holds.)"

2 Corinthians 10:3,4

Let's list some of our mighty weapons that become the ax in our hand to destroy the roots:

"Ye are of God, little children, and have overcome them: because greater is he that is in you, than he that is in the world."

1 John 4:4

We have to know that God in us is greater than the problem.

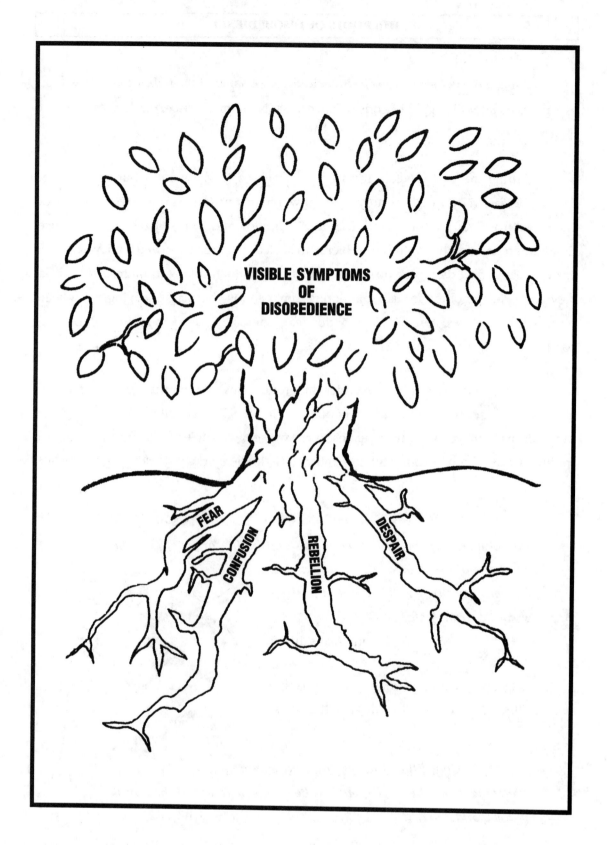

"And whatsoever ye shall ask in my name, that will I do, that the Father may be glorified in the Son. If ye shall ask any thing in my name, I will do it." John 14:13,14

We have the name of Jesus to use. Jesus stands behind that name, and God the Father stands behind that name.

"Wherefore God also hath highly exalted him, and given him a name which is above every name: That at the name of Jesus every knee should bow, of things in heaven, and things in earth, and things under the earth."

Philippians 2:9,10

Fear has to bow to the name of Jesus! Confusion has to bow to the name of Jesus! Rebellion has to bow to the name of Jesus! Despair has to bow to the name of Jesus! When a child walks into my classroom, he comes under my authority. As discussed in the previous chapter, Matthew 18:18 gives me the authority to bind away from the child the forces that are influencing his disobedience. Matthew 16:17,18 shows me I can have revealed knowledge of which forces are operating.

Warring in the spirit might sound something like this:

"Father God, I come to You in the mighty name of Jesus. I thank You that greater is He that is in me than he that is in the world. Father, I lift [insert child's name] before You. I take this opportunity to bind [insert name of force coming against the child] out of his life. I thank You that Your Word does not return to You void and that I have whatsoever I say. Thank You, Father. In Jesus' name."

You will need to use revelation knowledge to know what to pray for. Your prayer language is a great aid here. God may show you any number of problems to come against, but if there's any doubt about what specifically to pray for, a great work will be accomplished by covering the four main roots of fear, confusion, despair and rebellion.

After praying the above, I then take authority over any disobedience or strife, proclaiming that it will not come through the classroom doors, calling that territory "the anointed territory of God."

PREPARING THE GROUND

As you stand before your class and give God's Word, you are as a farmer sowing seed into the earth. Now the farmer wouldn't dream of walking up to a field covered in rocks, roots, and weeds and begin sowing seed. He must first prepare the ground. There is a lot of advance preparation and work needed. The land must be cleared of any hindering forces that keep the seed from finding good soil and taking root. So we need to do advance work and preparation to clear the ground in a child's heart so the "seed" can take root.

Here is a hypothetical example. Billy overhears his parents arguing over bills and other family problems. At night, after he goes to bed, he hears his parents battling again. This time, divorce is threatened in angry words. Billy is filled with fear and confusion about the future. He feels guilty for being a burden on his parents.

The next day, walking into your classroom, Billy is still troubled. He remembers the battle waging in his home. He is, essentially, like an overgrown field loaded with rocks and roots. No matter how exciting and inspired the message, Billy won't hear it. The seeds you try so diligently to sow won't take root and grow in Billy's heart.

But you, as Billy's teacher, can take authority. You can sweep away the debris of despair that clutches him. Billy will receive the message and the Word will take root.

THE MIRROR OF THE WORD

Billy needs more than the message, however. Billy needs to be handed the mirror of God's Word so he can begin to see himself through God's loving eyes. This is where confession plays a role.

One day, following God's direction in my own life, I sat down with a tape recorder and made a list of all the situations in my life that needed to be changed. I spoke God's Word into that tape recorder over each and every problem area. In the area of finances, I said, "Thank You, Father, that Your Word says that You want me to prosper and be in health. Thank You that I have whatsoever I say, and I say that all my needs are met, according to Your riches in glory."

In the end, I had recorded ninety minutes, confessing God's Word over situations in my life. I concluded the tape by recording a praise song and worshipping the Father. In my imagination, I could see Jesus up on a hill, sitting on a beautiful white horse, banners flowing, so majestic. I was in a crowd of thousands upon thousands. Each day I put that confession tape in my recorder, put on my ear phones and listened while I vacuumed and did the dishes. I confessed out loud what I heard my voice saying over all these situations.

After only two weeks of this, I had to make a new tape because eight major situations in my life had been totally turned around with the Word! Some of them had been strongholds for eighteen years. Those eight resolved trouble areas became praises at the beginning of the next tape.

One day as I was worshipping the Father, the Spirit of the Lord spoke to my heart and said, "Look where you are." In my mind's eye I was no longer in a crowd of thousands upon thousands. I was up on the hill, standing beside Jesus, worshipping the Father along with Him at His right side.

Now, it isn't that I had been confessing the Word for more than two weeks and had earned a place at His side. Jesus paid for that place long ago. "In Him," I was always at His side. Previously, I had taken shots at the enemy through my confession, but NOW I was picking up the mirror of the Word, and looking at myself through God's eyes instead of the world's. I had renewed my mind through the Word. My view of who I was, and Whose I was, had changed.

Increasing your understanding in this area will also increase the amount of authority in which you walk. Remember, you don't earn it. It's already yours. Take the victory that belongs to you.

Since this worked for me, I thought: wouldn't it also work for the kids? I brought a stack of blank cassette tapes to class, along with a typed confession that takes about five minutes to say. Each child recorded the confession which follows and rewards were given for those who repeated their confession daily, using the tape to help them along.

Step one is clearing the ground. Step two is fertilizing the soil, enriching the ground for a better crop. It gives the children a means to pick up the mirror of the Word daily. As they do, they begin to view themselves as valuable, precious and special to God.

Following these two steps will create a dramatic difference. The whole atmosphere of your classroom will change. You will find that it is not in taking the nose to the corner, but the heart to the throne that provides the answer to any discipline problem.

DAILY CONFESSION FOR CHILDREN

My name is _____. The Bible tells me that I am a child of God because I have given my heart to Jesus. As God's child, the Word tells me I am blessed.

It tells me that my angel stands before God daily.

If anyone offends me, it is better for him to be thrown into the sea with a millstone about his neck.

God tells me this because He wants me to know that He loves me.

He says that if anyone even gives me a cup of cold water, he will not lose his reward.

Jesus told the apostles to let me come to Him.

The Bible calls my praise perfect.

God loves children.

God chose Abraham because He knew he would teach his children.

David was just a boy when he killed a big giant, because God was big in David. God is bigger in me than any giant. In Jesus' name I can defeat all evil because God is big in me. God is bigger in me than any evil that would try to hurt me.

God spoke to Samuel and God speaks to me.

A child led Samson to the pillars of the Temple and I lead adults to Jesus. The Bible says, "a little child shall lead them."

God made all things and God made me. He made me in His image. I am a spirit. I have a soul, and I live in a body.

Jesus is preparing a place for me in heaven. Someday He will come for me and those I love and take us there. The streets are gold and it is a wonderful place.

I have on the armor of God:
- the helmet of salvation
- the breastplate of righteousness
- my loins are covered with truth
- my feet have on the gospel of peace
- I take the sword of the Spirit
- I hold up the shield of faith
- I have the name of Jesus in my mouth.

So, watch out, devil. I'm going to squash you under my feet!

HOW WE KNOW THAT
WE HAVE AUTHORITY

STUDY QUESTIONS FOR ADULTS (CHAPTER 3)

If I have spiritual authority, does it mean people have to obey me?

Jesus gave us authority over all **spiritual** forces (the power of the devil) that would try
to come against us.

Eph. 6:12,13 _____

Luke 10:19 _____

How do I know I have authority?

Matt. 28:18 (Jesus has it.) _____

Matt. 28:19 (He gave it to us.) _____

John 16:23-24 _____

Mark 16:15-18 _____

James 4:7 _____

Matt. 18:18 _____

Phil. 2:10 _____

Are you certain it will work?

John 16:33 _____

Why did God do this for me?

John 16:27 _____

CHAPTER FOUR

Following The Example Of Jesus

TEACHING CHILDREN IS MUCH LIKE BAKING A CAKE. You must have all the ingredients: your calling, the Word in your heart and the children to teach. Next, you need the proper utensils to prepare these ingredients: your training, an understanding of attention spans, an ability to tell stories, and other effective teaching skills. Then you must mix the ingredients together, pour it into a pan and put it in the oven. That's being a doer of the Word and putting into practice what you've learned.

All of the above will be to no avail if you haven't turned the oven on. You must have heat, or there will be no cake, no matter how carefully the ingredients have been mixed. *The heat is the Holy Spirit.*

When I grew up, we were really poor. I remember our oven never worked properly — and sometimes it didn't work at all! Even when the oven worked, it heated unevenly: you'd put a cake in to bake and it would come out lopsided. One side would be tall and moist, the other side would be like a crisp cookie.

We know that we must pray and seek the heart of God for our lessons, but often, we give God multiple choices: "Okay, God, do You want me to do this or that? Mark the proper box."

God is so good. He will lead us with whatever little bit of attention we give Him, but when we go to God for multiple choice answers, our "cakes" will bake, but with nowhere near the perfection they could have been.

One day, as I was kneeling down to "light the oven," I remained on my knees, seeking the Lord's guidance about an upcoming chapel I was to give at a local Christian school. I wasn't giving the Lord a multiple choice. I wanted His heart on the lesson.

Jesus said, "Get up, Charlotte," and as I obeyed, He asked, "Do you love Me?"

"Yes," I answered.

"Feed my sheep," He said.

"That's exactly what You said to Peter, Lord," I replied.

Jesus responded by saying, "My sheep are starving." He showed me I was to give the children *His heart,* not *my mind.*

"But, Lord, I am giving them what came from You," I protested, listing off the four lessons He had given me to share with the children about Design, Image, Guides and Eternal.

But the Lord said, "I'm going to teach you something."

Suddenly, I was in an audience. I was a child, with a child's view, watching me teach. This wasn't an open vision, but I saw it in my spirit. As clear and as real as the typewriter before me at this moment, I watched myself teach. And Jesus asked me what was happening.

Then it dawned on me. I became aware that there was a separation between myself as the child watching, and myself as the adult, teaching. I was surprised at the separation. It was as though, as a child, I was an observer, but not really a part of all that was going on. He showed me that this separation also existed in the spiritual realm.

Jesus then showed me how He ministered to the children:

"Then were there brought unto him little children, that he should put his HANDS ON THEM, and pray: and the disciples rebuked them. But Jesus said, Suffer little children, and forbid them not, TO COME UNTO ME: for of such is the kingdom of heaven. And he LAID HIS HANDS ON THEM, and departed thence" [author's emphasis].

Matthew 19:13-15

Mark's account in chapter 10:16 said that "HE TOOK THEM UP IN HIS ARMS, PUT HIS HANDS UPON THEM, and blessed them" [author's emphasis]. I could see Jesus say of the children, "Bring them to Me." He held them, hugged them, touched them.

Remember, all types of people came to hear Jesus, not just seekers of truth, but also curiosity seekers, Pharisees, and mockers. These children which Jesus brought into His embrace came from all kinds of backgrounds, and had all kinds of fathers. Jesus then showed me that when He hugged the children and gathered them to Himself, He was removing the sins of the fathers against them.

Jesus had taught me a lesson. I realized that the way to feed little lambs God's heart is to gather them to you, touch them, hug them, and love them.

Now I was ready to present the chapel service! The usual set-up was for the children to sit on bleachers in the gym, while I ministered from the center of the gym floor with a microphone. I asked the school administrator if we could do things a little differently this time. I wanted all the children seated, Indian-style, all around me on the floor.

Out of approximately three hundred children who attended the chapel that day, two hundred fifty gave their hearts to Jesus. Afterwards, filing past me on the way back to their classrooms, they were reaching out to touch my hand. Instead of smiling sweetly, as I would have done in the past, I drew them to me, hugged them and told them I loved them. No sooner than I'd hug one, than another would take his place, hungry for a hug also.

In my own children's church, which is much smaller than the 300 I taught that day in the chapel, I continued to put into practice those truths Jesus had shown me. Now I walk around the children's chairs as I tell them a story or preach. (Children need preaching, too.) I touch their heads, pat their shoulders, touch their hands. Hugs are handed out freely, and as they leave my class, each child receives a hug and I tell them I love them.

The little boys in the class are so cute. They pretend to be so tough. They lean into the hug, but act like they don't enjoy being hugged at all, but pressing into your arms. It makes me think of the scene from the movie "Snow White," when Grumpy receives his hug as he goes off to work. He enjoys it to the fullest, but grumbles under his breath so the other dwarfs won't think he's a sissy.

Father God was in heaven, teaching us through the law. Galatians 3:24 tells us that the law was our schoolmaster to bring us to Christ. We were separated from God by our iniquities, but Jesus put on flesh and became touchable, removing our iniquities from us.

"That which was from the beginning, which we have heard, which we have seen with our eyes, which we have looked upon, AND OUR HANDS HAVE HANDLED, of the Word of life..." [author's emphasis]

1 John 1:1

He removed the separation between God and man.

"But now in Christ Jesus ye who sometimes were far off are made nigh by the blood of Christ. For he is our peace, who hath made both one, and hath broken down the middle wall of partition between us."

Ephesians 2:13,14

We become one with Him, so close that we eat His flesh and drink His blood. He is our example of perfected ministry, speaking only the words He heard the Father speak, and touching, touching, touching — us.

Can you see the vicious attack Satan has perpetrated against the children? His plan is to isolate and separate them from the love and touch of God. "Beware! Beware of touches, beware of hugs, beware of strangers! Beware!"

We have children suspicious of loving hugs, and we have adults afraid to give those hugs, fearful of false accusations being made against them, making the children "untouchable."

"My sheep are starving."

How To Find The Lord's Heart On Children

STUDY QUESTIONS FOR ADULTS (CHAPTER 4)

What do I need to do to find the heart of God on a subject?

ABIDE

John 15:1-7 _____

ASK

Luke 11:9 _____

LISTEN

John 10:3-4 _____

What do I do after I find God's heart on the matter?

Do what He instructs.

James 1:22_____

If I obey God and it looks like things are not working out, what am I to do next?

Prov. 3:5-6_____

1 Peter 4:19_____

Psalm 116:17_____

CHAPTER FIVE

You Must Have A Servant's Heart

LET'S BEGIN BY LOOKING AT GEORGE WASHINGTON and his troops during the Revolutionary War. During the winter at Valley Forge, they lacked ammunition, food and clothing. The bitter cold was intensified by inadequate shelter. Thomas Paine was to write of this war: "These are the times that try men's souls." We've seen paintings depicting the men marching with bloodied feet, struggling to carry fellow soldiers who had been wounded or simply lost the will to continue.

As a little girl, when I would get hurt and cry, my grandmother would say, "Goodness gracious, girl, don't make such a rout. Soldiers in the war used to get their heads shot off and keep on marching." I used to wonder how they could see where they were going. My grandmother's keep-marching attitude came from the knowledge that the soldiers never gave up. There was a driving force that kept pushing them onward to victory. Those soldiers were fighting for freedom. It was very cut and dried, black and white. You fight, possibly die, so your children can be free. It was that simple.

By contrast, consider Vietnam, the longest war in which the United States ever took part. This war produced deserters, flag burning, protesting in the streets, low morale among the ranks, dissension, lack of unity, and bitterness.

The difference between Vietnam and previous wars was simple. This time, it wasn't cut and dried, black and white. Neither the soldiers on the front lines, nor the families back at home had a clear understanding of what the war was all about. The questions ran rampant, at home and abroad. What are we fighting for? What business do we have over there?

Clearly, the first thing necessary when preparing for battle is to have a good understanding of why you're fighting. You have to believe, without doubt, that what you are doing is valuable, important, essential. Otherwise, you'll end up with low morale, or even worse, deserters.

My family recently took a home-schooling field trip to Washington, D.C. We visited the National Gallery of Art. Among the many masterpieces on display was a painting by Rembrandt. A soft, black velvet rope draped through stanchions was all that separated us from this great work of art.

Fascinated by the detail and beauty, my teen-aged son reached forward to touch the painting. No sooner had his hand crossed the velvet rope, than a guard grabbed his wrist with a stern rebuke and moved my son's hand firmly back behind the rope barrier. I hadn't even noticed the guard before. But he had been there all along, protecting this masterpiece, a painting so valuable, so priceless, that it had its own guard protecting it.

Our heavenly Father views His children in the same way. They are so valuable, so precious, so special to Him that He has placed a guard around each one individually.

"Take heed that ye despise not one of these little ones; for I say unto you, That in heaven their angels do always behold the face of my Father which is in heaven."

Matthew 18:10

This scripture inspires a wholesome, fearful awe and respect for the responsibility God has placed in our hands when He entrusts His children to our care.

Meditate on this scripture for a while. You may not be as tempted to snap at Johnny for fidgeting or speak sharply to him when you're irritated.

"When the Son of man shall come in his glory, and all the holy angels with him, then shall he sit upon the throne of his glory: And before him shall be gathered all nations; and he shall separate them one from another, as a shepherd divideth his sheep from the goats: And he shall set the sheep on his right hand, but the goats on the left.

Then shall the King say unto them on his right hand, Come, ye blessed of my Father, inherit the kingdom prepared for you from the foundation of the world: For I was an hungred, and ye gave me meat: I was thirsty, and ye gave me drink: I was a stranger, and ye took me in: Naked, and ye clothed me: I was sick, and ye visited me: I was in prison, and ye came unto me.

Then shall the righteous answer him, saying, Lord, when saw we thee an hungred, and fed thee? or thirsty, and gave thee drink? When saw we thee a stranger, and took thee in? or naked, and clothed thee? Or when saw we thee sick, or in prison, and came unto thee?

And the King shall answer and say unto them, Verily I say unto you, Inasmuch as ye have done it unto one of the least of these my brethren, ye have done it unto me.

Then shall he say also unto them on the left hand, Depart from me, ye cursed, into everlasting fire, prepared for the devil and his angels: For I was an hungred, and ye gave me no meat: I was thirsty, and ye gave me no drink: I was a stranger, and ye took me not in: naked, and ye clothed me not: sick, and in prison, and ye visited me not.

Then shall they also answer him, saying, Lord, when saw we thee an hungred, or athirst, or a stranger, or naked, or sick, or in prison, and did not minister unto thee?

Then shall he answer them, saying, Verily I say unto you, Inasmuch as ye did it not to one of the least of these, ye did it not to me. And these shall go away into everlasting punishment: but the righteous into life eternal."

Matthew 25:31-46

Stop and consider Jesus' words, "Inasmuch as ye have done it unto one of the least of these my brethren, ye have done it unto me." Sunday morning rolls around. Through the doors of children's church bounces Suzie. She's saved and knows it, but is hungry for some meat from the Word.

Will Jesus be able to say to you, "I was hungry and you gave Me meat?"

Next comes Mary, thirsty for the Water of Life. Are you going to quench that thirst? Will Jesus be able to say to you, "I was thirsty and ye gave Me drink?"

Mary brought her little Mormon friend along, a stranger to the love of God. Are you able to take her in your arms and minister His love to her instead of criticize her? Will Jesus be able to say to you, "I was a stranger and ye took Me in?"

John walks through the door naked, his words revealing that he's not clothed with the robe of righteousness. Are you able to minister salvation, clothing him with the righteousness of Jesus Christ? Will Jesus be able to say to you, "I was naked and ye clothed Me?"

Mark and Joel are spitting and coughing with their little runny noses. Are you able to minister healing to them with the Word that's the answer to all sickness and disease? Will Jesus be able to say to you, "I was sick and ye visited Me?"

Carol and Don trudge through the door, imprisoned by fear and guilt and doubt. Do you, yourself, fully understand that God has not given us a spirit of fear "but of power, and of love, and of a sound mind"? Are you able to come into that classroom and greet those children prepared and ready to open prison doors? Will Jesus be able to say to you, "I was in prison and ye came unto Me?"

You need to fully understand that when those doors open, it is Jesus who walks through. Sunday morning, Jesus Christ will walk through your doors, wearing many different disguises, different faces. When you reach out and touch, you'll be touching Jesus. When snuggling a little child in a warm embrace, you'll be snuggling Jesus. *I'm* not saying this is so. Jesus says it is so.

Get this into your spirit, meditate on Jesus' words, and you'll never again feel that teaching your little class in the basement of your church is unimportant. You'll not grumble over preparation time or complain that you've been teaching six months without a break. You will see that what you're doing is valuable and important.

Children are not the Church of tomorrow. They are the Church of today. Satan doesn't sit back and say, "Let's not bother with Johnny, he's only a kid. We'll wait until he's a teen to bring attacks on him." No, Johnny is under attack from the womb. Satan tries to kill him through abortion before he ever sees the light of day. Then, after he's born, he's a target for everything Satan has, from AIDS to homelessness. Children need the Word of God from their mother's breast. (See Isaiah 28:9-10.)

When the apostles asked Jesus who was greatest in the kingdom of God, Jesus answered by sitting a little child in the midst of them. He then told them:

> *"Verily I say unto you, Except ye be converted, and become as little children, ye shall not enter into the kingdom of heaven...And whoso shall receive one such little child in my name receiveth me."*
>
> Matthew 18:3,5

What is the spiritual condition of our churches that we must beg for workers to help with the children? Could it be because there is usually very little praise for those who man the battle stations of the basement rooms? No limelight, no standing on a stage receiving the glory for our good works, no one to see our labors except Jesus?

Are God's people ready to get serious and really begin to serve Jesus? Are we ready to serve Him in secret, with no audience but Him? When we get that mind-set, it won't matter if no one ever notices what we're accomplishing with the children. It won't matter if the pastor and the congregation think we're only babysitting.

Children don't often walk up to you after service and say, "You were right on target with that message. It really ministered to me." You must sow the Word and know by faith that God's Word will not return to Him void.

To completely close every door to the enemy in the area of discouragement, you must not overlook the area of numbers. Now, to be certain, we want to minister to as many little ones as possible. But we don't want to fall into the world's trap of thinking bigger is better. This is not always the case. Philip was directed to travel a long distance out of his way to minister to one Ethiopian. Kenneth Copeland tells a story of God taking him all the way to Australia to minister to one lady in a restaurant. We don't want to be looking for the grand and miss the great. Satan will be robbed of the opportunity to discourage us when human recognition doesn't come, because we will be doing everything that we do as unto God and not unto men.

LEST WE FORGET

One additional thing I do to prevent discouragement is to write down the scriptures on ministering to children and review them often, lest I forget.

The Bible says God chose Abraham because He knew he would train his children (Genesis 18:18-19).

I remind myself that I won't lose my reward, even if I just give one of these little ones a cup of cold water in the name of a disciple (Matthew 10:42).

I remind myself that God calls their praise "perfect" (Matthew 21:16).

When the disciples tried to keep the children away from Jesus, He said, "forbid them not to come unto me; for of such is the kingdom of heaven" (Matthew 19:14).

I often remind myself that David was just a boy when he killed the giant, and Samuel was just a boy when God spoke to him. John the Baptist was filled with the Holy Spirit from his mother's womb.

OFFENDING THE LITTLE ONES

"But whoso shall offend one of these little ones which believe in me, it were better for him that a millstone were hanged about his neck, and that he were drowned in the depth of the sea. Woe unto the world because of offences! for it must needs be that offences come; but woe to that man by whom the offence cometh!"

Matthew 18:6,7

Hospital ministry allowed me to see the full consequences of offenses within the Church originating from people who have stood in leadership of the children. Probably a full 90 percent of the agnostics and atheists I met had come to their philosophy through two main roads: First, the Jews who had loved ones in the Holocaust; and second, by people who had been injured spiritually by a Sunday school teacher or religious leader. They had received the offense as coming from God, and as an adult, wanted nothing further to do with Him, if He even existed at all.

These offenses usually came as unkind remarks or touches that Satan made sure festered in the heart of the child until, as an adult, they chose never to be hurt again. In my hospital ministry, I would show the Jew from the Word that God not was behind the tragedy of the Holocaust, but instead that Satan was the guilty one. They usually came to Christ. But the one who had been offended as a child was much different. Those people were like immovable rocks, unwilling to hear anything from the God they felt had hurt or rejected them.

Children are like soft, pliable clay. They receive every impression you make on them. If you call them bad, they will receive that message, and perceive themselves as bad. You are the authority. You are telling them all about God. If you think they're bad, God must think they're bad, too.

Everywhere I go, I take opportunities to observe teachers in action. My heart burns when I have seen an irritated teacher dig fingernails into a little disobedient shoulder while directing them to their seat for the twentieth time, or when a frustrated teacher said, in front of the other children, "You always cause trouble."

The clay hardens and the impression is there forever, made by the hands representing Christ in the classroom. No wonder He says, "Woe to the one by whom the offense comes." God is love. He is kind and gentle and longsuffering. He is merciful. He wants to minister that love to the children through us. If we give the children anything other than the patience and love that He shows us, we are giving them a false god fashioned by our own hands. We are encouraging idol worship.

This doesn't mean we are not to correct children. The Word tells us He chastens the son He loves (Hebrews 12:6-8, Revelation 3:19). But there is a difference between godly correction and venting irritability and anger. If you've ever been guilty of that, ask God's forgiveness. Purpose in your heart never to do it again, and get on with the business of serving Him. Don't allow Satan to continually remind you of your mistakes. Pray for the one you've offended, and if the opportunity is there, ask him for forgiveness.

In the event you find yourself unable to control your emotions, children's church is not the place for you until you get this worked out in your life. The stakes are too high, the cargo too precious, and the time too short. The children must be able to step into your room and meet God. Nothing less will do.

A SERVANT'S HEART

Possibly there is a little more to preparing yourself for battle than you thought. Perhaps it's beginning to look like a lot of work. Let me tell you, it is a lot of work. In the natural realm, you'll be preparing lessons, making object lessons, making posters and puppets and anything else that will bring the message home to the children's hearts. And don't forget the other duties that accompany children's ministry: wiping runny noses, washing sticky hands, pulling gum off your new skirt.

In the spiritual realm, you'll prepare for battle by preparing the ground ahead of time and studying to become skilled in the Word. You not only need all of your Christian armor, but you must have, above all, a servant's heart.

Jesus tells us that "To become great in the kingdom of God we must become a servant" (Matthew 23:11).

My absolute favorite verses in the Bible are found in the Gospel of John.

"Jesus knowing that the Father had given all things into his hands, and that he was come from God, and went to God; He riseth from supper, and laid aside his garments; and took a towel and girded himself. After that he poureth water into a bason, and began to wash the disciples' feet, and to wipe them with the towel wherewith he was girded.

"So after he had washed their feet, and had taken his garments, and was set down again, he said unto them, Know ye what I have done to you? Ye call me Master and Lord: and ye say well; for so I am. If I then, your Lord and Master, have washed your feet; ye also ought to wash one another's feet. For I have given you an example, that ye should do as I have done to you." John 13:3-5, 12-15

Let's take a little closer look at these verses. It says Jesus knew who He was and whose He was. He wasn't groveling to find any small place in the Kingdom, just a cabin in the corner of Gloryland. He knew full well exactly who he was. Just as He had laid aside His heavenly body to put on human flesh, He was now laying aside His garments and girding Himself with a towel.

Jesus also poured His own water. Often, in children's ministry, depending on the size of your church and your pastor's heart towards children's ministry, you may have to come up with your own tools and supplies. But you can always trust God to supply what you need.

Once, I needed sponge to make seven puppets. I said in my heart, "Father, I need enough foam to make seven puppets. Let's see, I need a piece about six feet by two feet, about one inch thick." Then, recalculating after remembering I needed foam for the chests, too, I added, "Oh, yes, and a few more feet for the chests."

I never spoke this aloud to a soul. I didn't even officially pray for the foam. I was just conversing in my mind with the Father. I said, "Well, God, if You want me to have the foam, You're going to have to supply it. It's Your ministry, not mine." Then I forgot about it.

We lived about forty-five minutes from church, and just a few blocks from our house, my husband suddenly stopped the car. It was dark and I couldn't see what he was after as he began to back up. (Gil frequently brakes for turtles, rescuing them from an uncertain fate, depositing them in the nearest canal. Living in the country, this happens often.) I thought, "There he goes again, risking all our lives, stopping in the middle of the road, to save another turtle."

But soon, he opened the door and pulled into the car a spotlessly white piece of sponge. Its dimensions were six feet by two feet, one inch thick! Then, he pulled in another piece, three feet by two feet, the perfect size for the chests.

"Where do you suppose that came from," Gil mused.

I was beside myself with joy! I was screaming and shouting and praising God! "I'll tell you where it came from! It dropped straight out of heaven! I ordered it just as we left church."

See what I mean? God will supply all your needs!

After pouring the water in the basin, our Lord began to wash the disciples' feet. Scripture shows us that Judas was one of those disciples and that Jesus already knew that Judas would betray Him. Yet He washed Judas' feet also. He didn't say, "I'll get you later. Boy, are you going to be sorry when my Father gets His hands on you." He simply washed his feet the same as if he were John, the disciple whom Jesus loved.

So we see that from Jesus' example, our servanthood is not dependent upon the worthiness of those we serve. It is not dependent upon whether they love us or not. It is not dependent upon whether we agree with how they live their lives. We serve because Jesus served, and commanded us to do likewise.

Note that Jesus did not wipe their feet with a separate towel, but instead used the towel with which He was girded. This signifies He was clothed with the garments of service. Jesus did take back His regular clothes again and sat down as Master and Lord. But first, HE HAD TO BECOME A SERVANT.

To become great in the kingdom, we must become a servant. In all of the ministries in the church, you will never find a field richer with opportunity to become a servant than you will find in children's ministry.

Our Father has made it very clear to us that the children are to be taught. (See Deuteronomy 4:10, Genesis 18:19, Deuteronomy 6:7, Proverbs 22:6, Isaiah 28:9-10, Deuteronomy 11:18-21.) Given the nature, the maturity level and the energy of the children, it takes someone with a servant's heart to do the job well. Knowing full well who you are, and whose you are, look into the mirror of His Word. See that without you, and others like you, the children will perish.

No ifs, ands or buts: it's black and white, cut and dried. You will see yourself as valuable, precious, important and special to God because He has entrusted to you His most valuable, precious, important and special treasures, His children. Only then will you be truly prepared for battle.

GOD REWARDS THOSE WHO SERVE

STUDY QUESTIONS FOR ADULTS (CHAPTER 5)

How do I know that God sees all that I do?

Psalm 139:7-8 _____

1 Cor. 4:5 _____

How do I know that I will be rewarded?

Heb. 11:6 _____

Rev. 22:12 _____

Gen. 15:1 _____

1 Cor. 2:9 _____

CHAPTER SIX

Four Areas Children Must Understand

PAUL SAYS IN 2 CORINTHIANS 11:3, "But I fear, lest by any means, as the serpent beguiled Eve through his subtilty, so your minds should be corrupted from the simplicity that is in Christ."

There are four main areas in which children need to be taught. The Lord summed these areas up for me in four words: Design, Image, Guides, and Eternal. If you instill in a child knowledge in these four areas, you will have done a mighty work in the life of that child. Let's take a closer look at each of these four areas.

Design: A heart-felt knowledge that he was designed by God.

Image: A clear understanding that he was designed in God's image (spirit, soul and body)

Guides: An understanding that God wants to guide him and a knowledge of how to receive that guidance.

Eternal: A view of the eternal, teaching him to be heavenly minded.

Within the context of these four areas of instruction, you will have covered salvation, receiving the Holy Spirit and walking in the Spirit.

Only while writing this book did I begin to realize that each one of these four areas work to combat one of the roots of disobedience: Fear, Confusion, Rebellion and Despair.

Fear is combatted with the acceptance of knowledge of a great Designer who is on their side and loves them. When we first moved to the country, my daughter, Angie, was just six years old. She already had a real heart knowledge of God as her Father, and she didn't doubt for a minute the power of the name of Jesus. While fishing at the canal beside our home, a pit bull charged her, growling with bared teeth. She spun around, pointed at the dog that was just a couple feet away, and with great authority, commanded, "In the name of Jesus, you get away!"

That dog acted like it had been hit with buckshot! Tucking its tail between its legs, it turned and ran away, yelping and whining. The children who were with Angie came running to tell me. They had never seen anything like that. Angie just took it for granted and went on fishing. But she had no fear because she knew that the Greater One was dwelling within her. Knowledge of the Designer eliminated any fear.

Confusion is dispelled with the clear understanding that we are created in God's image. Confusion is also associated with other destructive emotions such as anger and self-doubt. Here is an example. My home schooling material includes a high school-level book on logic and higher-level thinking skills. Glancing through it one day, I came across a series of pictures, covering two pages.

The first picture was a stick drawing of a person's face. It was captioned, "This is a tubble." The first drawing was followed by seven or eight more, each labeled as "a tubble" or "not a tubble." The final drawing carried the question, "Is this a tubble?" Obviously, the first drawings were to enable the student to draw a conclusion about the last drawing.

I pondered over that question. It confused me. I could find no way to answer it. I turned the book over, rechecking on the cover the grade level. I was filled with self-doubt. What's wrong with me? Any high school kid should be able to do this. Why can't I?

The more I tried, the more confusing the problem became. I started getting angry. I reasoned with myself, "This is ridiculous! There is no answer! Put the book down. It must be a misprint."

Just then, Jacob, my eight-year-old son, leaned over my shoulder, read the pictures aloud, and when he came to the final question, answered without hesitation, "Yes." As he started to walk away, I called him back.

"Wait a minute, Jacob," I said. "Why did you answer 'Yes'? I've been looking at this for twenty minutes. I can't tell if it's a tubble or not."

"It's easy," Jacob replied. "Tubbles have no straight lines."

Sure enough, after Jacob walked away, I looked at the drawings again and saw that he was right. Every tubble had been formed with curved lines. Suddenly, it was clear and simple. I was no longer angry or confused. With understanding, came a clear mind.

Rebellion is abated by seeing that God wants to guide them to freedom. Often, children have a misconception of God as a hard task-master. He stands with a whip, demanding they follow Him. "Sit up straight! Eat your spinach! Go to Africa and be a missionary." It is possible that their earthly fathers have fostered such images in their minds.

Doing our job successfully, we will help nurture a fellowship between the children and their Heavenly Father and will disclose Him for who He is — loving, kind, gentle, giving and not taking, only wanting what is for their benefit.

If you effectively present the truth to the children that God's boundaries are love and His guidance the only true freedom, they are able to grasp and understand.

Lastly, **despair** disappears with the reality that an eternal home actually does exist.

The Church in the last few years has concentrated heavily on victorious living and being overcomers. Praise God for that! We don't have to wait for the sweet by and by to be blessed. But to be victorious and to be an overcomer, you have to have something to be victorious over and something to overcome.

We all know what that is. It's tribulation. Tribulations are like my laundry. No matter how much I wash, fold and put away, there's always a new batch tomorrow.

Jesus promised us that we would have tribulations in this world (John 16:33), but we are "to be of good cheer" because He also tells us, "I have overcome the world."

The amount of cheer you are experiencing in the midst of those tribulations will depend on the degree to which you are believing God's Word at any given time. On a child's road to becoming a strong believer who is victorious in every circumstance, they need to know that this world, with all its tribulations, is not the final word.

I remember an incident in my class a few years ago. It was the Christmas season. My lesson was all prepared with some wonderful dynamite truths from the Word. There was a boy in the class named Bobby. It was his second time with us. Just as I started into the lesson, Bobby raised his hand and pointed to the manger scene. "What's that?" he asked.

I made him point again and repeat his question. I just couldn't believe that this child didn't know about the manger. As I questioned him, I learned the awful truth. Not only did this young child not know about the manger, he had never been told the story of the birth of Baby Jesus. He had no idea who the people were who were depicted in the scene.

The dynamic truths I had prepared for the day were set aside. Instead, I taught the most dynamic truth of all, the simple story of how Jesus came to earth to rescue us from our sin.

A child must first be born again if he is to be able to receive even the most simple of truths. So stick to the plan, plain and simple. You'll get the job done right.

THE GOSPEL IS SIMPLE

STUDY QUESTIONS FOR ADULTS (CHAPTER 6)

SALVATION

How do I know that Jesus wants every person to be saved?

2 Peter 3:9 _____

Luke 19:10 _____

Luke 15:7 _____

Why are so many people not saved?

2 Cor. 4:4 _____

Eph. 4:18 _____

What can I do?

Pray using your authority. Command the scales to come off their eyes and that they come to the knowledge of the truth.

Matt. 18:18 _____

2 Cor. 4:6 _____

Believe they will receive the words you speak as coming from God. Expect them to receive as the Holy Spirit communicates the love of the Father through you.

John 12:32 _____

Mark 11:23-24 _____

Personalize the Gospel. Use their name as you share.

Romans 3:23-24 _____

John 3:16 _____

Point out the difference between religion and relationship.

John 4:23-24 _____

Simplify it.

2 Cor. 11:3_____

It is so easy. Confess and believe and be saved.

Romans 10:9-10 _____

For future sin

Leave them scripture to stand on for assurance that God will always forgive them. Their salvation is based on the Blood of Jesus not their failures or successes.

1 John 1:9 _____

Romans 8:1 _____

Eph. 1:4_____

Do not forget to give them their change of address.

Eph. 2:6_____

CHAPTER SEVEN

Children Are Designed By God

ASK ANY LITTLE ONE IN YOUR CHILDREN'S CHURCH, "Who made you?" and you will get a parroted reply, "God made me." Usually, children will repeat this fact long before it becomes revelation knowledge in their hearts. Our job is to help make that fact real to them.

To do so, we must first understand the tremendous pressures coming against the mind of the child. The same way that the Word of God is a seed of faith, Satan's words are seeds of doubt, planted with the purpose of bringing disbelief. Schools teach evolution as fact, instead of theory. Television programs, from sit-coms to nature and wildlife programs, are saturated with evolutionary teachings and assumptions.

When a child enters your room, he has been deluged with doubt and disbelief. You cannot expect him simply to accept on blind faith the fact that "God made me." Each little person needs to be equipped with the knowledge of truth.

When teaching children about creation, teach them from every angle. Cover all the bases, leaving no door open for the enemy. Give them all the answers before the questions are even asked! I begin first in the Word, using the Genesis account of creation.

THE LIE OF EVOLUTION

When you speak of evolution, use the word "lie." It is the "lie of evolution," a lie from the lips of the father of lies.

You can't repeat or emphasize this too often. Make them hear it so much that when they're back in their school classrooms and hear the word "evolution," they automatically think "lie."

Speak of those who believe the lie as those who are deceived.

It is good to use posters and other visual materials. God has blessed me with the gift of an artist's ability and I use illustrations whenever possible. But if you can't draw, find someone who can, or cut pictures from magazines. Children retain more if they can see as well as hear. Top retention comes from doing as well as seeing and hearing.

Here are a few examples of activities you can do to drive the truth home.

Activity — An Accidental Tapestry

Give each child in the room a spool of thread and tell them to toss their spools into the air at the count of three. Repeat this several times. Hold up a piece of cloth woven into a beautiful design. Ask the children how many times they think they would have to toss their spools into the air before the threads would all mesh together into a beautiful piece of cloth.

The children, of course, will say, "It will never happen."

But argue with them. Say, "Oh, yes! I know I can do it. I bet if I throw these threads up four thousand times, they will come down looking like this perfect piece of cloth."

They will begin to hoot, laugh, and shout, saying it's impossible. You can take this opportunity to show the children that this is exactly the nonsense the evolutionists are trying to make them believe about creation. Could the beautiful design of the universe just have happened accidentally? Over and over, I tell children a simple truth: Where there is a design, there has to be a Designer!

Tell the children, "You wouldn't walk over to this beautiful piece of cloth and say, 'Oh, look what happened.' Instead, you would say, 'Oh, look what somebody made.'"

My son owned a hand-held magnifying light that enlarged objects to thirty times their normal size. I brought this to class and allowed each child to examine the fabric of their clothing with this device.

It enlarged the threads to look like giant cords woven into a perfect pattern. This seemed to impress them as much as anything that we did.

Just keep making the children aware of the patterns and designs around them and reminding them that where they see design, there is always a Designer. Here are a few more examples of activities that teach this same thought to intersperse throughout the lessons on Design.

Activity — A Randomly Constructed Rocket Ship

Part of the decorations of your room could be a fully assembled rocket ship and a box of junk. This box of junk can be thrown into the air like the thread, only this time, trying to see if it will come down into a perfectly formed rocket ship.

This is an excellent time to show the children, from a library book, a magnified view of the retina of an eye. The thousands of rods that receive light are an awesome view of our Master's handiwork.

Activity — Writing an Encyclopedia — the Easy Way

The same thing can be done with a box of letters, seeing if they come down as a book of the encyclopedia. The examples are endless. The more the better. Keep them displayed to remind the children of the absurdity of the evolutionists' claims. Each time, remind them that when we see design, we know there is a Designer.

When I was preparing to teach on this subject, my son's school science book was a great resource. It taught the law of entropy, stating that disorder naturally increases.

Activity — The Law of Entropy

I took some pool balls and put them on the table, held by the little triangular frame.

"Children," I asked, "when I move this frame away and use a pool stick and ball to hit these balls, what do you think will happen?"

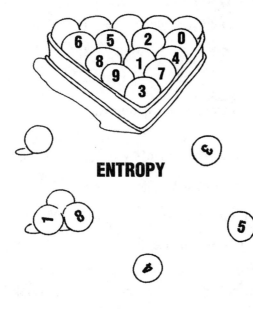

ENTROPY

The children responded that the balls would go all over the table.

But just as I baited them about the thread, I began to argue that the balls would scatter, then draw together again into a perfect triangle. Kids love to argue and they shouted, "No way, no way."

When they were all worked up trying to convince me it was impossible, I told them they were right. (Kids also love to be right!) Then I told them about the law of entropy.

Next, I pointed out that evolutionists ignore this law, and say that all matter was once a tiny ball that became unstable and exploded forming our planets. Show how silly this "Big Bang" theory is, how impossible for something to explode then become orderly again. Explain how stupid Satan thinks they are to believe such a lie.

When my son was younger, he asked for a huge eight-foot inflatable dinosaur for Christmas. Normally, this request would have been set aside for something a little more useful and lasting, but I was about to teach on evolution and knew he would let me borrow it, so the purchase was made. I also found some dinosaur key chains and dinosaur rings and erasers for just pennies each from a wholesale novelty gift catalog for give-away prizes.

The class was decorated with my other son's dinosaur collection. The inflatable dinosaur hung from the center of the room. Posters added to the atmosphere, creating the feeling you were stepping into the past when you entered the room.

I should note that I leave posters from previous lessons hanging around the room as a review and a visual reminder that design equals Designer, and that threads don't accidentally form a beautiful piece of cloth. Leave your object lessons on display as a constant reminder of what they've learned.

Ask the children what they would do to find out the truth if they didn't know God or know about the Bible. They will probably say they would do scientific experiments. Show them that scientific experimentation has proven that the evolution theory is a lie. Living things come only from living things, not from some Big Bang.

Activity — Living Things Come from Living Things

Some scientists believe in evolution because they believe that living things can come from non-living things. This belief, called "spontaneous generation," came from seeing flies seemingly come from decaying meat and frogs crawling from the mud.

Tell the children about a scientist named Francesco Redi. He performed experiments, stretching gauze over a jar of decaying meat and observing flies laying eggs on the gauze and maggots hatching on the gauze. This proved that the life did not come from the decaying matter, but rather from the living fly.

Using plastic meat and plastic flies, duplicate this experiment for the children. Ask, "Weren't they silly, children, to think that the flies came from the meat? Isn't it sad for evolutionists to believe we came from a big bang? We need to pray for the evolutionists. They should go to school, read in their seventh-grade science books about Francesco Redi, and learn the truth."

TRUTHS THE BIBLE TOLD FIRST

Better yet, these scientists could have saved themselves a lot of time and trouble by just reading the Bible. It has told the truth all along — long before scientists ever discovered it. The Bible is the most scientifically perfect book in the world.

Activity — The Foundation of the Earth

Almost two thousand years *before* Christ was born, the Bible told us that the crust of the earth rests upon a foundation (Job 38:4-6, Psalm 104:5).

Science finally discovered this in 1935, almost two thousand years *after* Christ was born. The Bible was four thousand years ahead of science.

When you point this out to your class, you can say, "See? If scientists would read their Bibles, they would save themselves a lot of work, and find the true answers."

Display a fish bowl or some other see-through container with rock on the bottom and different layers of earth on top. (If you are unable to do this, copy the drawing above onto a poster board.)

Label the fish bowl with appropriate scriptures.

Keep this on display during the weeks you are covering the lessons on Design. Review it often.

Activity — The Singing Stars

The Bible told us two thousand years before Baby Jesus was born that stars produce sound (Job 38:7). Science finally accepted this in 1942, almost two thousand years after the birth of Baby Jesus. Again, the Bible was four thousand years ahead of science.

Make a poster of the singing stars (copy my drawing if you wish), or use a Christmas tree star that makes music when plugged in. Label the star with appropriate scriptures. Be sure to display this, also, throughout the lessons on Design. The star and fish bowl could be labeled with appropriate scriptures.

Activity — The Life is in the Blood

The Bible told us in Leviticus 17:11 (written about 1425 B.C.) that the blood sustains life. Science didn't accept this until 1900 A.D.

This time, the Bible was thirty-three hundred years ahead of scientific investigation. Again, scientists could have saved themselves a great deal of money, experimentation and frustration if they had gone to the source, God's Word, for the answers.

You may copy the sample picture onto a poster or display blood some other way. One example would be the pumping hearts that you put together. They can be found in toy departments, usually in the same area where microscopes, ant farms and other scientific toys are displayed. Another way would be to show a toy hypodermic needle from a toy doctor's kit. Some show the blood by having a tube inside that is painted red.

Activity — Oceans Have Currents

The Bible told us in Psalm 8:8 (written in 1000 B.C.) that ocean currents flow through the seas. Science accepted this fact in 1855 A.D. The Bible knew about the currents twenty-eight hundred years ahead of science. Smart people go to the Bible. Smart people know where the truth is found. Smart people listen to God's Word.

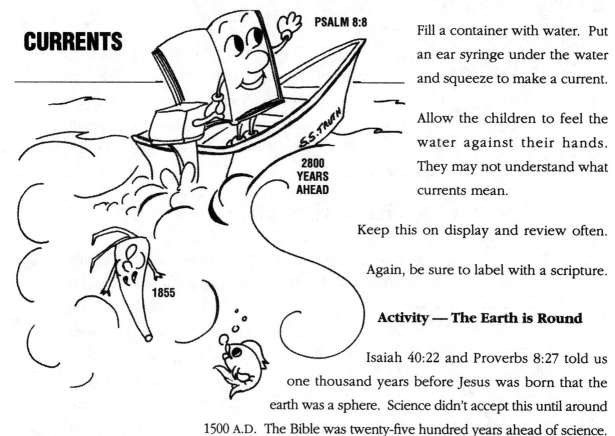

CURRENTS

PSALM 8:8

S.S. TRUTH

2800 YEARS AHEAD

1855

Fill a container with water. Put an ear syringe under the water and squeeze to make a current.

Allow the children to feel the water against their hands. They may not understand what currents mean.

Keep this on display and review often.

Again, be sure to label with a scripture.

Activity — The Earth is Round

Isaiah 40:22 and Proverbs 8:27 told us one thousand years before Jesus was born that the earth was a sphere. Science didn't accept this until around 1500 A.D. The Bible was twenty-five hundred years ahead of science.

Job 26:7 (written around 2,000 B.C.) tells us that the earth is suspended in space. This was accepted by science in 1687 A.D. The Bible is first again, this time by some thirty-six hundred years.

How silly we are when we search everywhere else for the truth but the Bible. Smart people believe the Bible. Someday all the scientists will listen to the Bible. Many scientists already are smart. They say that evolution is a lie and the Bible is true. We don't have to wait four thousand years, or twenty-six hundred years, or even

SPHERE SUSPENDED

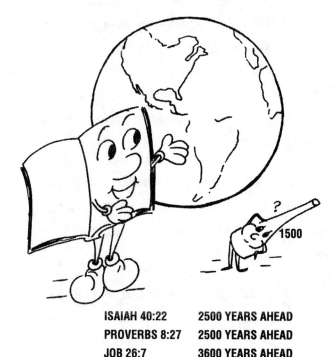

ISAIAH 40:22	2500 YEARS AHEAD
PROVERBS 8:27	2500 YEARS AHEAD
JOB 26:7	3600 YEARS AHEAD

one year. We can be smart right now. We can believe the Bible.

Use a giant, blow-up globe hanging from the corner of the room.

Write across it the appropriate scripture.

If you are unable to use a globe, copy the sample picture provided.

Keep it on display and review it often.

Seeing all these truths magnifies God's Word to the child. It makes the Word bigger, larger. You want the Word to dwell big in the hearts of the children. The more visuals you use, the more effective your lesson will be. As you scan through library books, encyclopedias and school books, the Holy Spirit will bring alive wonderful object lessons.

Using markers and flannel, you can make custom-made flannel graphs for this lesson. (I ironed some Stitch Witchery between two pieces of flannel to make mine a little sturdier.) Again, if you can't draw, cut pictures from a picture book and glue them to the flannel. Where there is a will, there is a way!

Puppets are a favorite part of any lesson. Kids relate to puppets. When they see their favorite character overcome their problems with God's Word, it encourages them to do the same. They think, "Gee, if a puppet can do it, I can do it."

Whatever tools you use, puppets, object lessons, posters or flannels, have the children repeat the truths you have taught. "So you see, children, design equals Designer. Say this after me: Design equals Designer." It is important that they say it with their own lips. It is easier to embrace and make the truth your own when you speak it.

Activity — Mrs. Radio

Mrs. Radio is one of the favorites of the children in my class. She is simply a cardboard box large enough for my tape player to fit inside. Covered with metallic wrapping paper, her eyes and mouth are glued on and her nose is a radio dial. The recorder is set on play, and while plugging in the recorder, I pretend to be setting the nose dial and tuning her in.

I have prerecorded the story with some actual radio static in the beginning. And then Mrs. Radio takes over: "Good morning, boys and girls. This is Mrs. Radio, with another exciting story from God's Word."

MRS. RADIO

The story is told and Mrs. Radio brings home the truth: "Boy, that was a close one, boys and girls. Jeremy almost believed the lie Satan tried to tell him. Don't you fall for his tricks. You believe God's Word. This is Mrs. Radio, saying good-bye until next week."

Most of my materials I pick up at garage sales. If I wait until I need something for a lesson I'll be teaching that week, forget it! I'd never find what I need! Some things I've found months in advance of when they would be used.

Another way to accumulate materials you need for your lessons is to put a notice in your church bulletin, listing the different items you will need. A member may have just what you need to make your lesson come alive, and may be more than happy to donate it.

Be as creative as you can. With the help of the Holy Spirit you'll come up with ideas that you never would have thought of on your own.

Keep presenting the same truth over and over in different ways. When that child leaves your room in a few weeks, he will know that he knows that he knows that evolution is the lie and that the Bible is true and that design equals Designer. You will have accomplished what you set out to do. "God made me," will not just be a parroted response, but rather true revelation knowledge in the heart of that child. That is a truth that the gates of hell will not be able to come against.

WE ARE DESIGNED TO BE HIS TEMPLE

STUDY QUESTIONS FOR ADULTS (CHAPTER 7)

How does the Holy Spirit help me think of ways to present His Word?

Prov. 8:12 _____

2 Tim. 1:14 _____

John 14:26 _____

I know it was a work of the Holy Spirit that saved me, but can I have more?

John 16:7 _____

Acts 1:8 _____

Acts 19:2-7 _____

Will the Father give the Holy Spirit to me?

Luke 11:9-13 _____

ASK HIM!

> Father, I ask You in faith for Your gift of the precious Holy Spirit. You
> promised Him to me, so I receive the blessing that is mine as Your child.
> I am now filled with Your Spirit and will speak to You in other tongues.
> In Jesus' name. Amen.

Mark 16:17 _____

Eph. 5:18 _____

Acts 2:1-4 _____

Acts 8:14-19 _____

Isaiah 28:11-12 _____

Acts 10:44-46 _____

Luke 24:49 _____

Gal. 3:14 _____

CHAPTER EIGHT

Children Are Made In His Image

Y ou have completed the lessons on Design. The children know, without a doubt, that they have been designed by the Great Designer. While studying "Image," the children must see that of all things God created, they are different.

As a teenager, I remember sitting with my mother at our kitchen table, looking down at a single drawing on a paper napkin. With just a few strokes of her pen, along with her short explanation, it was suddenly as if the fog lifted. All the puzzle pieces fell into place and understanding came. The Bible no longer was mysterious and hard to understand.

I understood salvation and being Spirit-filled like never before. Now there was no doubt in my mind about the difference between religion and relationship. Law and Grace, Old and New Testament suddenly were joined in one harmonious cord of love. I would never think of myself in the same way again.

THE TEMPLE OF GOD

Leviticus 16 explains the once-a-year blood sacrifice, made by the high priest for the sins of the people. This yearly sacrifice was made in a special part of the tabernacle (and later the temple in Jerusalem) known as the Holy of Holies. Both the Tabernacle of Moses and the temple in Jerusalem consisted of the outer court, the inner court and the Holy of Holies.

Anyone was welcome in the outer court. This is the place where the money changers had been selling sacrificial animals and Jesus drove them out. But the inner court was for Jews only. Within this inner court was the Holy of Holies. Between the inner court and the Holy of Holies hung a huge, four-inch-thick veil which reached from the high ceiling to the floor and from wall to wall. Only the high priest was allowed in the Holy Place to offer sacrifice for the sins of the people.

There were bells on the bottom of his robe that made a tinkling sound when he walked, and a rope was tied to his leg, with the other end left outside the curtain. If the people stopped hearing the little bells, they would know he had entered "unclean" and died. Even then, the people were not allowed to go in and bring him out. Instead they would pull on the rope to haul him out from the Holy of Holies.

In the Holy of Holies, the high priest would sacrifice a perfect lamb, without spot or blemish, to pay for the sins of the people for another year. The ark of the covenant rested in the Holy of Holies. On the ark were two angels of gold, whose wings touched in the center. It was here that God spoke to His people.

The temple was the house of God. This temple, made with hands, was built of specific size and dimension, according to God's direction. It was a three part building, symbolizing the Triune God. The temple was a shadow of the building that was to house God in the future, one not made with human hands.

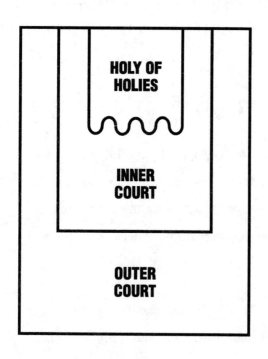

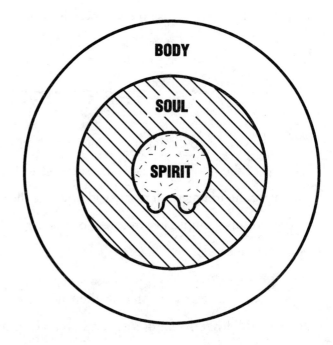

THE NEW TESTAMENT TEMPLE

Just as the temple was three parts, we are a three-part being. In I Thessalonians 5:23 we read, "...and I pray God your whole SPIRIT and SOUL and BODY be preserved blameless unto the coming of our Lord Jesus Christ" (author's emphasis).

The outer court of the temple was open to all, just as our equivalent of the outer court, our bodies, are also open to all. (I can like you or not like you and it doesn't keep you from seeing that I have black hair or red hair, brown eyes or blue, that I'm tall or short. This part of me is open to all.)

Just as the temple had an inner court, open only to the Jews, I have an inner court, my soul. Not every passerby knows what I am thinking. I only open my soul to special ones whom I have chosen.

My spirit is a reflection of the Holy of Holies. This is the part of us we struggle to understand. Some even spend thousands of dollars on psychiatrists, attempting to find the meaning behind their actions. But it's money down the drain. No one has the right to enter this holy place except our High Priest, Jesus Christ.

We find in John's Gospel the story of the woman at the well. In John 4:20 she has asked Jesus where men ought to worship. He replied, "Woman, believe me, the hour cometh, when ye shall neither in this mountain, nor yet at Jerusalem, worship the Father." He was telling her that the world was about to have a new place of worship. In verse 23 He said,

"But the hour cometh, and now is, when the true worshippers shall worship the Father in spirit and in truth: for the Father seeketh such to worship Him. God is a Spirit: and they that worship him must worship him in spirit and in truth."

This woman had just perceived that Jesus was a prophet and now He stood prophesying to her, not only of an hour that was to come, but is now standing in her presence.

The end of the Old Testament was about to come. The New Testament stood before her. Jesus ministered under the old covenant and kept all the laws. His birth did not close the last book of the Old Testament. His death did. The place of worship, the house of God was about to be changed from a temple built with hands to a new temple, not made with human hands.

When the spotless lamb, Jesus, was sacrificed for the sins of the people, it was the final sacrifice. There could be no more sacrifice for sins. For what could be a greater sacrifice than the Son of the Living God? Here we find the true end of the Old Testament:

"And Jesus cried with a loud voice, and gave up the ghost. And the veil of the temple was rent in twain from the top to the bottom."

Mark 15:37,38

There was to be no more sacrifice in this man-made temple, for God Himself had torn open the veil separating us from Him. He accepted the last sacrifice made for the sins of man.

When we accept that sacrifice, we are born again. We become the new house of God. We become walking, breathing, moving temples of God when we are filled to over-flowing with the baptism of the Holy Spirit.

"And what agreement hath the temple of God with idols? for ye are the temple of the living God; as God hath said, I will dwell in them, and walk in them; and I will be their God, and they shall be my people."

II Corinthians 6:16

Our worship must come from within our hearts. The new covenant is now in effect and in fact must dwell within us to be worship at all.

"Woe unto you, scribes and Pharisees, hypocrites! for ye are like unto whited sepulchres, which indeed appear beautiful outward, but are within full of dead men's bones, and of all uncleanness. Even so ye also outwardly appear righteous unto men, but within ye are full of hypocrisy and iniquity."

Matthew 23:27,28

We can now see the true problem of the hypocrites. They simply cleaned up the wrong part. That is how good church members, or even pastors, can one day run away with the church secretary: they've cleaned up the outside, but not the uncleanness of their hearts.

FROM A CHILD'S VIEW

Although my mother's explanation brought me great understanding, keep in mind that I was a teenager when she told me these things. Now I needed to deliver this message in a way that would be easily understood by young children between the ages of six and eleven.

With the help of the Holy Spirit, I believe I have discovered the best way to teach this lesson. My kids have a thorough understanding that they are spirits, having souls, living in bodies. I use this lesson as a pivoting point of many others. When trying to make a point on another subject, I refer back to this lesson and it brings understanding.

Activity — Spirit, Soul and Body

(If you can get adult volunteers for this lesson, it's even better. If not, please be careful to never cast a child in the role of a sinner. Make sure you pick a different name than any of the children in your class. Then, explain to the class that the children holding the props would never do anything like you will be talking about. Remind them they are just holding the props.)

Stand three people of the same sex in front of the room. Label one "spirit," one "soul" and the other "body." Add the props to each child as you teach on each one. Explain to the children that when you look at Suzie, you only see her body, but introduce them to her soul and spirit.

Tell the children that Suzie has a problem. *Walk over to the "spirit" person. Show them the sinful heart and death reigning. (I use a black felt heart and a ferocious looking plastic dinosaur.)*

Then walk over to the "body" person. Tell the children that the people who meet Suzie think they know exactly what Suzie's problem is. Some say Suzie has a problem because she drinks Burpie beer. *(Use a soda can with a pretend label.)* Some people think it's because she smokes cigarettes. *(Roll a piece of white paper around some polyester stuffing. Pull a little of the stuffing out one end and color it red.)* One person is sure it's because she's a Playboy bunny *(she puts on a white wig with bunny ears)* and she gambles *(use some large dice).*

Have another person play the role of God. Keep referring back to the "spirit" person, pointing out it is the only place God is looking. *Have "God" stand beside the "spirit" person and just keep looking at him.* Explain that God only looks at the heart. All God sees is the sin and death reigning.

Suzie's body went to church one day and naturally, her soul and spirit went along, too, because they are inside Suzie's body. Suzie heard the preacher say that you need to ask Jesus to come into your heart and clean you up and start living for God so you can go to heaven. She only heard part of what the preacher said. She wasn't paying close attention. All Suzie heard was that you need to clean up your life. She missed the part about Jesus coming into your heart and that He is the one who cleans you up.

Suzie set about the task of trying to do something about her life. First, she quit her job at the Playboy Club *(take off the wig).* Next, she quit gambling and drinking Burpie Beer *(remove the dice and beer can).* Last of all, and hardest of all, she used all her will-power and quit smoking *(remove cigarette).*

People started noticing Suzie. They started to say to each other, "Have you seen Suzie lately? She's really changing. She doesn't smoke or drink anymore. Wow!"

But look, boys and girls. See where God is looking? He's still looking at Suzie's heart. God can't see any change because He only looks at the heart.

Suzie started looking around her at all the other people in the church and she saw how they were acting and decided that she needed to change even more. Suzie got a big Bible *(hand a Bible to the "body")*. She bought a great big cross to hang around her neck *(hang foil cross around "body")*. Suzie went to Bible school and got a diploma *(hand the "body" an over-sized diploma)* and she received "Best Student of the Year" award *(pin to "body")*. Suzie even started paying her tithes *(I use a 20-inch fake dollar bill for this)*.

Now everyone is really impressed with how much Suzie has changed. *(Pretend you are one of the people and walk around the "body")* Say, "Oh, look at Suzie. She is sooooo spiritual. I wish I were like her. She reads her Bible, pays her tithes, goes to Sunday school, etc."

But boys and girls, look at God. Where is God still looking? What does God still see? He only sees a black heart and death reigning.

Thank God, Suzie's grandmother prays for her every day and when Suzie was in church one Sunday morning, she heard everything the preacher said. This time, she heard him say that you need to ask Jesus into your life and let Him clean you up. Thank God, she heard that, boys and girls, because you know what all of her efforts to clean herself up looked like to God? He says our righteousness is "as filthy rags." *(Wrap Suzie's body in a dirty black cloth filled with rips and holes)*. It was ugly to God.

Suzie prayed the prayer, and asked Jesus into her life. He removed the old black heart of sin and replaced it with a new heart *(red felt heart)*. Death no longer reigned in her life because Jesus said, "I am come that they might have life, and that they might have it more abundantly" (John 10:10). *(Toss away the dinosaur.)*

Jesus wrapped Suzie in His robe of righteousness. *(Wrap this around the "Spirit" person. I made a gold lame cape with white silk lining and white fur trim for this.)*

Jesus crowned her with a crown because she is going to rule and reign with Him. *(Put a gold crown on the "spirit.")*

Now what does God see, boys and girls? And now that Suzie's heart is cleaned up God's way, He can look over here at her body and see the things Suzie has done. He will reward her for her hard work, but all those things she did to her body wouldn't help Suzie get to heaven.

I gathered my props for this from various places. You don't need to use the same ones I did. You could use a rubber snake to represent sin or a white sheet for your robe of righteousness.

We made paper dolls to allow the children to teach this lesson to their friends and parents and to keep the truth before their eyes after they left our room. I have included patterns for you to copy and use.

Give the children a chance to respond to this message. (In fact, give the children an opportunity to respond to every message you give!)

Ask them if they have ever asked Jesus to come into their hearts and remove that old black heart of sin. Ask them if they have ever been wrapped in His robe of righteousness.

(Be sure you have allowed any children who were standing to sit down. This gives them a chance to respond also.)

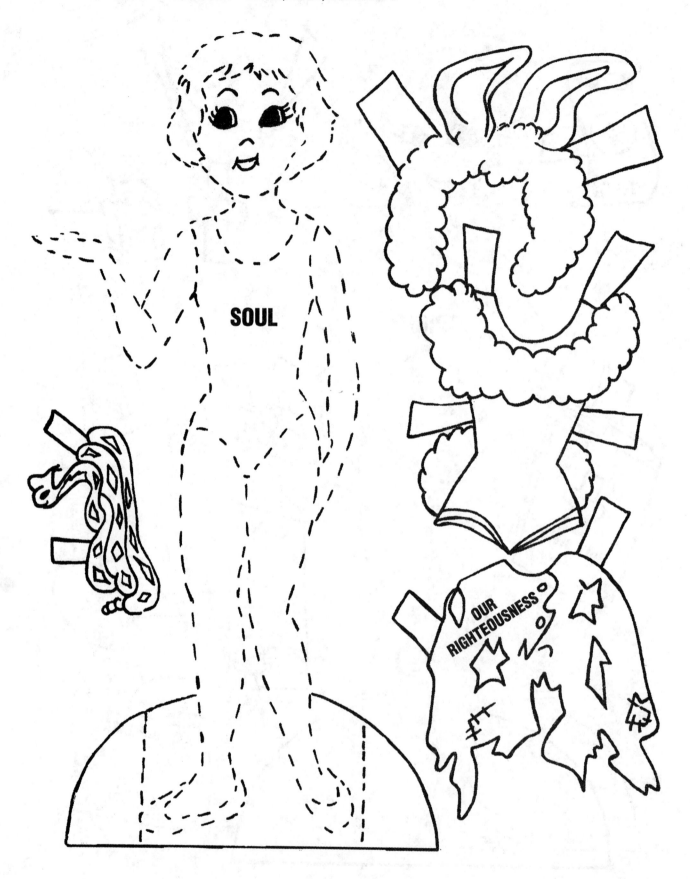

BODY

CLEAN HEART

ALWAYS POINT TO THE ANSWER

Never, never, never point out sin and bring a child under conviction without offering the answer to the sin problem.

This happened to me when I was just seven years old. The traditional religion I was in pointed out my sin to me and the consequence of that sin, without giving me answers. I was terrified. They told me God saw through walls and knew everything I did. I knew I couldn't quit sinning, so I figured I had better make friends with the devil so he wouldn't burn me.

At the age of seven, I actually told the devil he could have my soul. I told him that I would be his wife. At that moment I made that pact, a heavy mirror fell over and came within an inch of killing me. Thank God I had a praying grandpa who lifted me to the throne daily. The angels were watching over me and kept me safe until, at the age of eight, I discovered the love of God.

This lesson can be added upon, line by line, precept by precept. I used building blocks to actually build a small temple with the two courts and the Holy of Holies. We tore a veil and used a manger-scene lamb to show the sacrifice. Friends of mine have made a papier-mâché lamb filled with red ink. They used this as an object lesson of the spotless lamb being slain for our sins.

Activity — The Soul Man's Role

Invariably, the question arises, "What happens to the soul?" I made a head piece that looks like the brain and put this on the person, explaining that this is the seat of the mind, will, and emotions. The "soul" man gets covered with various props to reflect this: math flash cards to reflect intellect, a black and white card to represent choosing between good and evil, water for tears of emotion, and so on.

Activity — Renewing the Mind

You can glue all types of props to small clothespins and attach them to the mind. Use Tylenol bottles, movie advertisements, etc. to represent the world's view. Small Bibles, army men and other objects can be used to represent God's view of filling themselves with the Word, renewing their minds.

This activity explains working out the soul's salvation with fear and trembling.

Activity — Cares and Worries

In one lesson, I hung a heavy weight around the soul's neck and called it "cares and worries." Then I attached a rubber steak to it and labeled it "lion meat." Satan goes about as a roaring lion, seeking whom he may devour. Cares and worries are so heavy that they weaken our souls and welcome attack.

As children thoroughly understand these truths, you can take them into deeper truths. The applications are endless. Your children end up with a deeper understanding of the Word than most adults sitting in the pews of adult church.

GOD IN THREE PERSONS

When you are teaching this lesson, be sure to spend sufficient time on the Trinity. Although this is a difficult concept that defies the understanding of even the most intelligent scholars, make an attempt at bringing a better understanding to the children. As I mentioned earlier, having a clear understanding of themselves as being created in God's image will help dispel confusion.

The following is a puppet skit God gave me to help the children understand the implications of His three-fold being.

PUPPET SKIT: THE MASTER PLAN

Puppets Needed: Devil, Demon, Angel

Subject: The Trinity

Time: Christmas

(Music opening as Devil and Demon enter)

Devil: Ha! Ha! Ha! Ha! I love it! I love it! I'm so wonderfully wicked, I scare myself. This is the most sinister plot I've ever slithered into.

Demon: What is it, Master?

Devil: It's the best one yet!

Demon: I don't know, your Evilness. What could be any better than when you deceived those dummies in the garden, Alex and Effie?

Devil: Speaking of dummies, it's Adam and Eve, not Alex and Effie...!

Demon: Oh, yeah, Adam and Eve. Anyway, that was pretty evil, getting them to disobey God and give the authority of the Earth over to you.

Devil: Oh, my new plan is more evil than that! This plan is fantastically fiendish.

Demon: But your Grand Filthiness, sir? What could be more fantastically fiendish than making the Israelites forget God and worship the Golden Calf after all He had brought them through?

Devil: All that was just baby stuff compared to this master plan. Ha! Ha! Ha! Ha!

Demon: The Golden Calf, baby stuff?

Devil: You bet! I'm going to use God's own...yuk Word...to take over heaven as well as Earth. Then I'LL BE GOD!

Demon: But how?

Devil: I'm going to take over His throne! Ha! Ha! Ha!

Demon: Easier said than done, Master. God sits right now, this very minute on His throne. He's ruling. You can't get God to get off the throne. Besides that, He's stronger than you. If you tried to get Him off His throne, He'd punch your lights out. Oh, excuse me, your Awfulness, I mean He'd punch your darkness out.

Devil: Listen, stupid...I know He's stronger, but I'm going to trick Him. You see, ever since Alex and Effie..., I mean Adam and Eve. Drat it, now you've got me doing it. Anyway, since I deceived them, I've held all of mankind in bondage. Ha! Ha! Ha! Ha!

Demon: Yeah. Ain't it fun?

Devil: Stick around kid. It's gonna be a lot more fun. I've found out God's weakness

Demon: Oh, goodie, goodie!

Devil: What!

Demon: Oops! I mean, baddie, baddie!

Devil: That's better. God's weakness is He always keeps His Word!

Demon: Where does He keep it? Are we gonna steal it?

Devil: No, dingy, He keeps it, He keeps it. That means if He promises to do something, He does it, no matter what. And, in His Word, I saw something that is going to be His undoing. See, I have everyone trapped in sin, right?

Demon: Right, Master.

Devil: Well, He promised man that He would come to Earth and save them. He doesn't have sin, so He's the only one who can do it. So that's my plan. Isn't it great?

Demon: What's so great about Him rescuing people from sin? I don't understand.

Devil: You dummy! Then He leaves heaven and goes to Earth to rescue men, I'm gonna hop on His throne and take over heaven. THEN I'LL BE GOD!!

Demon: I love it! I love it! This is a MASTER PLAN, Master!

Devil: Of course it is! Ha! Ha! Ha! Ha!

(They continue their evil laughter as they exit.)

(Christmas background music as angel and shepherd enter.)

Angel: Fear not; for behold I bring you good tidings of great joy, which shall be to all people. For unto you is born this day in the city of David, a Savior, which is Christ the Lord.

              And this shall be a sign unto you; ye shall find the babe wrapped in swaddling clothes, lying in a manger.

(Angel and shepherd exit, Christmas music fades out.)

(Demon and Devil enter to some dreary sounding music.)

Devil: I can't stand it! I can't stand it! Foiled again!!!

Demon: But Master? Your plan worked. You heard the angel. God came to Earth. He's a baby over there in that manger. Now is your big chance. You can take over heaven.

Devil: First off, I don't listen to angels. Secondly, something has gone wrong. I can't figure it out! That can't be God over there in that stable!

Demon: Why not, master?

Devil: Because He's STILL ON HIS THRONE!!! I can't figure this out. How could He be both here and there at the same time? This is terrible, terrible, terrible!

(The devil wails as he exits.)

Demon: Come on, Master. We'll roast some marshmallows and think up another master plan.

(Demon exits as music fades out.)

You will notice that I always use a confused, stupid, bumbling Devil. The point to get across to the children is that there is a force out there who is trying to influence them away from God. Always make the devil the loser. He is always failing and running in fear.

It's not necessary to terrorize children with the devil to get them to follow God. Jesus said, "If I be lifted up, I will draw all men unto Me." Lifting up and magnifying the devil is not how we get people drawn to Jesus. So lift up Jesus and put down the devil. That's where he is anyway...under your feet!

I Am Made In His Image

STUDY QUESTIONS FOR ADULTS (CHAPTER 8)

Now that we are saved and Spirit-filled what does the Word have to say about us?

We are "in Him."

Acts 17:28_____

We are seated in heavenly places.

Eph. 2:1 _____

Eph. 2:4-6_____

We are new creatures.

Eph. 2:10 _____

2 Cor. 5:17 _____

We are forgiven.

Rom. 8:1_____

We are delivered.

Col. 1:13-14 _____

Eph. 1:7 _____

Rom. 8:2_____

We are healed.

1 Peter 2:24 _____

Matt. 8:17_____

Gal. 3:13_____

We are prosperous.

Phil. 4:19 _____

3 John 2 _____

Luke 6:38 _____

CHAPTER NINE

Children Need God's Guidance

My heart is filled with such joy at the thought of sharing this portion of the teaching with you. In my mind's eye, I can just see each of you taking this lesson into your classes and the little children walking out knowing the voice of God.

My mother was a wise woman. Many people came to her for advice and counsel. It was amazing to me how many of them wanted to know what they should do about this job, or that problem. Most of them were seeking answers from a person, rather than the Person.

Thank God, my mother was a godly woman who had no intention of trying to push God off the throne to sit in His place. Instead, she taught people to hear from God themselves. This often took longer than just handing out advice. But in the long run, the rewards were far greater.

"For as many as are led by the Spirit of God, they are the sons of God."

Romans 8:14

"And when he putteth forth his own sheep, he goeth before them, and the sheep follow him: for they know his voice." John 10:4

"Behold, I stand at the door, and knock: if any man hear my voice, and open the door, I will come in to him, and will sup with him, and he with me." Revelations 3:20

Scripture shows us, without a doubt, that He wants to guide us. We are fully capable of receiving that guidance. We have been made capable through Christ. We have been made sons of God. Jesus is the Great Shepherd, and we are the sheep of His pasture.

"I WILL SUP WITH HIM"

As we embark on this study to understand how to hear from God, it's important to remind ourselves that we are not working formulas that will bring down the mighty voice of God on our humble beings. He has chosen to call us no longer servants, but friends. We are going to begin to fine tune our understanding of our precious friend that already is living within us. He wants our fellowship to be as intimate as our relationship. He wants to come in and sup with us.

Yesterday, I was having tea with a friend. We laughed as we spoke of some of the funny things that had happened in our lives. Hopes, dreams, and desires were discussed. Encouragements were exchanged. As she left, we hugged. I was left with a warm, happy feeling of peace and contentment.

Jesus says that He will "come in and sup with us." He means exactly the same type of fellowship as with a friend who sits at your table for tea. He cares about your hopes, dreams and desires. He wants to encourage you and lift you up. He always leaves you with a peace and contentment that no earthly friend could ever give.

Our goal should be to instill this same kind of fellowship with God in the children we teach. We must be certain they realize they don't have to become "good enough" to make God talk to them. Jesus did it all. We simply have to receive what He already has done.

When I first taught on this subject, I gathered everything I could from great men of God. Kenneth Hagin has a book, *How to be Led by the Spirit of God*, that was a wonderful resource. I also used an article from a Kenneth Copeland publication, *Inward Witness*. It is important that along with the Word, you gather as much inspired information as possible. Enrich yourself in any area that you teach. Put it all in, stir it up with prayer, and allow the Holy Spirit to bring out what He desires for the children.

There are three main ways that God guides us. First is the inward witness. This is the principal way He guides us. Next is the inward voice, and third is the voice of God. And there are three stages for teaching children to be guided by God. The first is to get them to recognize that they have spiritual feelings that are different from their five senses.

84

Secondly, they need to determine whether the feeling gives them a STOP or a GO inside. Finally, they will be ready to learn not just to hear the STOP and GO, but how to receive detailed directions from within.

THE INWARD WITNESS

"The Spirit itself beareth witness with our spirit, that we are the children of God."

Romans 8:16

Activity — Learning to Listen for His Voice

A good way to explain hearing from their heavenly Father is to turn on a radio or cassette player and set the volume very low. Make it so low that they can hardly hear it. Tell them that God is already talking to them, but that they are not accustomed to listening for His voice, so they may not be able to hear it clearly. Like the sound of the radio, explain that as they begin to practice listening for the guidance from their spirit, they will begin to hear better. As this point, raise the volume of the radio. Pretty soon, they will be able to hear His voice more clearly than their own. Raise the volume to a loud level.

Activity — Soft or Scratchy?

Show the children a piece of steel wool and a piece of soft fur. Allow them each to feel the scratchy steel wool and the soft fur. Ask them to explain how differently the two objects feel. Tell them that deep within them, they have feelings that come from their spirit. When people say certain things, they either get a good feeling, like the soft fur, or a scratchy, bad feeling, like the steel wool.

Say a few extreme things, allowing the children to close their eyes and identify which feeling they got with the words. Is it scratchy and bad, or soft and good? You might say, "God loves you and wants you to be well," or "God hates you and wants you to be sick." Point out that they immediately could identify the scratchy bad feelings when the lie about God was said.

When the children have learned to quickly identify the spiritual feeling, begin to make the statements a little less extreme and the lie a little more subtle. Try a statement such as, "God loves you, but He's going to make you sick to teach you something." I have yet to do this with a class that they didn't immediately recognize a scratchy feeling after that statement. Sometimes the children hadn't even had teaching in that area, yet still they knew something was wrong with the statement.

Activity — Red Light or Green Light?

I learned part of this technique from *Super Church Curriculum* by Mark Harper.

Use a poster-board picture of a traffic signal to identify the "Stop" or "Go" from within. I drew a picture that actually shows a traffic light coming from within the child's tummy area (see illustration).

Next, teach the children to recognize a STOP or a GO, a YES or a NO. Tell them to look in the same area as the steel wool feelings and the furry feelings to see if the traffic light within was on green for go or red for stop. Again, here you start with extreme statements that are easily identified as red or green. Move on to the more subtle statements as the children become more skilled at identifying the traffic signals.

INWARD WITNESS

I was able to purchase a large traffic light from Radio Shack. Loosening the bulbs, I let each child have a turn tightening the green bulb for go and the red for stop, according to what they were feeling as a witness from within for each statement.

Once, I asked the children what they would do if they were playing on the playground and a good Christian friend of theirs asked them to come over and play at their house. Chris, the youngest boy in my class, four at the time, raised his hand and ran to the traffic light. He immediately turned on the yellow caution bulb and said, "Yellow, because even though he's nice, your mother might not know where you are." Chris was ready for stage three, getting specific guidance from within.

GETTING GUIDANCE FROM GOD

In stage three, the children learn that they can find guidance from God in the same place their inner "traffic light" is located.

Activity — Hearing God's Plan for Me

Tell the children, "God is speaking to each of you. Just as you looked within for the traffic light, you will now look in the same place to see what God is speaking to your spirit." Tell them God has a plan for each of their lives. They don't have to wait until they are all grown up to find out what He wants to say to them right now.

Have the children close their eyes and begin to wait on the Lord.

When I did this in my class, after just a few minutes, one boy raised his hand and said, "God said He wants me to be a scientist for Him."

I praised him and said how wonderful that was. A few minutes later, a child said, "God wants me to be a preacher."

There was a new girl in our class. She'd only been to children's church a couple of times. Her mother was a bar maid and a drug addict. She had no father. A friend was bringing her to class. Shyly, she raised her hand and said, "God wants me to be a barmaid."

She barely finished the word "barmaid" when I shouted with much enthusiasm, "Wonderfullllll!" I knew I had to rescue her before there could be a laugh or a snicker. A situation like that could keep her from ever wanting to try and hear from God again.

As I stretched out the word "wonderful," I called in my mind, "Help, Jesus. I need wisdom." And then it came. "Do you know why that is wonderful? It shows you have a servant's heart. The more time you spend in children's church and the more you practice hearing from God, you will see that He will be showing you a better way to serve people. There was a beautiful woman who had a servant's heart like you do. Her name was Florence Nightingale..." By the time I finished telling them about Florence Nightingale, the other children had forgotten the little girl's reply.

Just like a baby falls many times before beginning to walk, the children will have their ups and downs also. The thing to remember is that we're not out trying to win any race, just patiently training them in the way that they should go. Depending on the age division of your children's church, you could have that child for up to six years. Be patient and don't dig up your seed to see if there are any roots yet. Don't force a child who isn't ready. You can kill the seed that way.

Activity — Puppet Slide Show on Hearing from God

My own children went with me to the zoo, along with my puppets. Using a 35mm camera, we took slides of the puppets acting out a story. The children held the puppets in the poses, outside the view of the camera and we got some beautiful shots. In the story,

Jeremy finds a watch that another puppet loses. For each time he received the inward witness telling him to return the watch, the devil tried to talk him into keeping it.

I took a picture of a real traffic light. As we move from cage to cage, Jeremy's spirit is dealing with him. In the end, he listens to his spirit, returns the watch and receives a reward.

That Sunday, we used a slide projector as I told the children the story. They were thrilled. It was just another way to present the truths being taught.

The more visuals you use when teaching, the easier it is for the child to grasp the concepts taught, and remember them.

INWARD VOICE

The second way we are guided by God is through our conscience, or the voice of our reborn spirit called the *inward voice*.

"And Paul, earnestly beholding the council, said, Men and brethren, I have lived in all good conscience before God unto this day."

Acts 23:1

"Now the Spirit speaketh expressly, that in the latter times some shall depart from the faith, giving heed to seducing spirits, and doctrines of devils; Speaking lies in hypocrisy; having their conscience seared with a hot iron."

I Timothy 4:1,2

Activity — Learning to Tell Conscience from Condemnation

Tell the children that even people who are not born again have a conscience. Explain to the children that their conscience had been made new when they were born again. God will use their conscience to guide them. A person who is not born again might not have their conscience bother them if they cuss. A new creature in Christ will feel the prick of their conscience when they do the former things.

Be very clear in the difference between conscience and condemnation. Explain it to the children this way: "Boys and girls, let's say that your mother tells you to pull weeds from the garden. Instead of doing it, you go outside to play. Each time you pass the garden, your conscience might tell you, 'You should pull the weeds in the garden because you are to obey your parents.' That is good for your conscience to guide you in this way. Your conscience is trying to get you to obey.

"The Bible tells you to obey our parents. But sometimes the devil will try and disguise his voice to sound like our conscience and bring condemnation on us. He might put a thought in your mind like this. 'You should have obeyed and pulled the weeds in the garden. You didn't because you're just a no good person. Your mom and dad don't like you anymore because you never obey.' Do you see the difference? The second voice wasn't trying to get you to obey. The second voice was trying to make you feel ugly and unloved. That voice came from your mind, not your spirit. That is called condemnation.

"God loves us even if we don't always obey. He wants us to be happy and lead a peaceful life. That is why He tells us to obey. We should obey our conscience."

Activity — Soft Heart or Hard Heart?

Used a sponge heart painted red to represent the tender conscience. Give each child a chance to have a squeeze. For the conscience that had been seared with a hot iron, I used a heart-shaped red paperweight. You could use hardened clay or simply knock on a hard surface while explaining how hard it is for the hardened heart to receive the gentle prodding of the precious Holy Spirit. The children could each knock on their own chair.

FINDING THE PROPS

In my home, I have almost a whole room full of various paraphernalia to use for object lessons and illustrated sermons. Some of the items are quite elaborate and expensive, like the traffic light. But I wasn't blessed with such an array of visual aids overnight.

There is a tendency sometimes to hear of the great things people are doing with children and get discouraged because you think, "I could never afford to do that with my class." But don't become discouraged and as the Bible says, don't despise small beginnings!

When I first started teaching children about listening to their heart, I used a construction paper heart. After that, I made a poster board one, with a painted smiley face glued to a Popsicle stick. Then, a few months later, I made a stuffed one from fabric and glued on moveable eyes. Eventually, I made my wonderful heart puppet that I am presently using. The last few weeks, it has been stirring around in my spirit to make a huge heart costume that a helper could wear. I can just envision my heart coming into the room and pulling me away from some dumb temptation like stealing a piece of candy.

The important thing is to work with what you have. The Holy Spirit can work on a heart without one prop from you. Trust God to do the very best you can with what's available. It's taken me five years to collect the items that fill my room. Most either came from garage sales or were donated. At one point, I asked the congregation for any weird items they might have from plastic fruit to old wigs.

The different holidays are a wonderful time to shop around for unique object lesson items that you might have trouble finding at other times of the year. To illustrate the voice of the Spirit of God, I use a pretty white dove that I purchased in a craft store around Christmas time.

During Halloween, I purchased a rubber devil. He has many uses. Whenever I'm showing a child tempted to do wrong, I show this rubber devil whispering in his ear. Sometimes we speak the Word and throw him in the pit. Other times he's great for just stomping on. He has been curled up and put in a plastic heart to show that "Out of the abundance of the heart the mouth speaketh," and sometimes he hides behind a light, disguising a lie with some truth.

Valentine's Day is great for all types of hearts, plastic see-through, hard hearts, heart-shaped cookie cutters, etc. Christmas is the best of all. Tree ornaments and other decorations have endless possibilities, everything from guardian angels to forbidden fruit.

When I'm out shopping, I keep my eyes open for anything that might have to do with upcoming lessons. A fabric shop had material filled with bright traffic signals and road signs. A small piece of this made great bean bags for quiet-seat prizes. Another time, I found a small plastic traffic light on a key chain. I even found some gaudy traffic-signal earrings, which I wore to class while teaching the lesson.

The idea is to do whatever you can to keep the lesson before their eyes, especially after they leave the classroom. Crafts and small projects are important, as they reinforce the lesson. We simply color the picture of the traffic signal coming from the belly and then glue red glitter on the red light. I like to ask the children, "Now, when you go home today and your Mom and Dad ask you why the traffic light is coming from a little girl's tummy, what will you answer?" This is a good way to find out if they understood the lesson. It's also a quick review before they leave the class.

Emphasize how important it is to hang their project on the refrigerator or set it on their dresser. I tell the children that each time they look at their craft, the Holy Spirit will quicken the truths to them over and over.

We went to camp meeting in Tulsa and stayed with our friends. Their daughter, who had been in my class for years before they moved, handed me a present just before we returned home It was a paper craft that we had made in my class probably three years earlier. What a blessing!

THE VOICE OF THE SPIRIT OF GOD

Finally, God sometimes speaks to His people through the voice of the Spirit of God. This is the least common way that He speaks to His people today. In the Old Testament, it happened all the time. Moses heard a voice from a burning bush. Samuel heard this voice when he thought Eli was calling him.

But now God dwells in His people. He has given us a new heart. We don't have to wait for a burning bush to hear from our Father. Although God at times still speaks to people in this manner, this does not happen too often. Yet some people are waiting for a burning-bush experience to be able to know God's will for their lives.

The voice of the Spirit of God does not come through your ears, although it may seem as though it does. God is a Spirit. The spirit of man is the candle of the Lord. He communicates through our spirit when He talks in this manner. His voice is much more authoritative than the voice of our reborn spirit.

Let me give you an example in my own life. I had purposed in my heart that I was going to spend quality time with God. The children were small and two were still in diapers. With five children, a mother doesn't get a lot of time alone to pray and meditate the Word. The kids were always up by 6:00 or 6:30 a.m. So I set my alarm for 5:00 a.m. The first couple of mornings, I did great. It was so wonderful having sweet fellowship with Him before I had to face the crying and fussing, the dishes, etc.

This particular morning, I was really enjoying my sleep. The alarm sounded and I just reached out and turned it off. The air was a little chilly and the comforter was so warm and snuggly. I just rolled up a little tighter and started to go back to sleep. The voice of the Spirit of God gently said, "Get up, Charlotte." It seemed audible, almost like a whisper. Yet I knew it came through my spirit. I whined, "But I'm so comfortable. I can't get up. I'm too tired."

Let me tell you what had happened just before I went to sleep the night before. I had been reading an article about watching for the coming of the Lord. Those who were caught sleeping were going to be taken by surprise and those who were watching and praying were going to be ready for His coming. As I went to sleep, I had been musing over in my mind to the Lord, "Am I going to be one of those caught sleeping? I hope not, Lord. I want to be ready when You come."

So here I am the next morning, resisting the voice of God gently prodding me awake. This time a little louder and with more authority, "Get up, Charlotte." This happened three times, while I laid there, unable to respond, totally ruled by my slovenly flesh. Silence. I drifted back to sleep.

Suddenly, I heard a blast of a trumpet at my ear, so loud it sounded like dynamite set off in my eardrum. My body went straight up in the air. I was on my feet in one terrorized leap. I stood, bent at the waist, with my feet planted about three feet apart on the floor. My heart was pounding so hard that my throat ached. The realization hit me that my husband was still sleeping peacefully in bed. He hadn't moved. I could see the cribs and the children's beds from where I stood. Not one of them had heard a sound. None of them stirred either. As I stood there, clutching my heart, breathing hard and trying to figure out what had happened, the Spirit of God said, "See, Charlotte, you won't be caught sleeping because you obey My voice."

I can laugh at this now as I see God has a sense of humor. But at the time, it put the fear of God into me. Now you might say, "Oh, this lady sounds like some kind of flake." But didn't He say He would come in and make His abode with us? He is very real. He is not a storybook character. He is alive. He promises to never leave us or forsake us. He is our forever friend.

GIFTS OF THE SPIRIT

I don't want to leave the subject of guidance without mentioning the gifts of the Spirit. God speaks to us through the gifts. But do not get into this now with the children. Wait until you are teaching a series on the gifts. Before you teach on any of the ways He communicates with us, be certain you are familiar with all the ways.

An example is the Word of Knowledge. For a little over a year, I did hospital ministry two times a week. One time, the nurses asked me to take Gabrielle, my angel puppet, in to cheer up a man who was really bad off. They explained that he had been in a head-on collision and that his pregnant wife had been killed. His six-year-old daughter, who was in the back seat, had survived and was in the pediatrics ward.

This man had so many bandages, casts, tubes and tractions it was unbelievable. They said they had given him medication for pain but that each time one of them came into the room, he would begin to thrash in the bed and make grunting sounds, looking pleadingly like he was trying to tell them something. At first, they were concerned that the man was experiencing horrible pain. But then they noticed that as soon as they left the room, the thrashing stopped. Due to his serious injuries, the man was unable to talk.

After hearing the background, I took the puppet into the room. Sure enough, as soon as he saw me, he began to thrash back and forth and make grunting noises. Walking up to him, I told him to be calm, everything was going to be okay, and that I came to pray for him. Laying hands on him, I began to pray, in my prayer language. I didn't know where to begin to pray because he was in such serious condition. Immediately he grew still. Leaning over, I asked him if he was a Christian.

"Blink once if you are," I directed. He blinked.

"Are you spirit-filled?" He blinked again.

I explained to the man that the nurses were concerned because they couldn't understand what he was trying to say. But, I explained, that the same Holy Spirit who lived in him also lived in me. The Holy Spirit would tell me what he was trying to say. I left him with that promise.

All the way back to church I was praying in my prayer language for the man. It was about a 45-minute trip. When I was almost to the church, I suddenly knew what he was trying to say. The word of knowledge just came to me.

Hurrying to the nearest phone booth, I called the nurses. "Have you told him yet that his wife and baby are dead, but that his little girl survived," I asked. They said they hadn't, afraid that he wasn't strong enough yet to take the news. They felt his condition might worsen if they let him know. I told them very boldly what I had promised their patient, and how I had prayed. I explained that the Lord had shown me he was trying to find out about his wife. The torment of not knowing was doing him far more harm than the knowing.

Without hesitation, the nurses said they would tell him immediately. The next time I went into the hospital, the nurses met me with the news that I had been correct. As soon as they told the man the news, he never again thrashed in the bed or grunted. The man eventually recovered, having fully depended upon God for the peace that he needed.

His little girl, however, hadn't spoken a word since the day of the accident. She was recovering physically, but no matter how hard everyone tried, they had been unable to get her to say a word. They thought perhaps my angel puppet might stir her into responding.

She was a precious little black girl with the cutest little braids. As I entered the room, she glanced my way and proceeded to ignore me, continuing to watch her television, while running her hands up and down the metal bars of her crib-like bed. I was praying for Father to give me wisdom as I endeavored to catch her attention with the puppet. She wasn't even slightly interested.

Finally, I introduced myself, took off the puppet, set it aside, and told her I didn't really like puppets that much, either. I told her that I had really come to find someone to play a couple of games with me. All this time, I was crying out in my heart for help and didn't cease to pray in my prayer language.

She continued to ignore me, as I started playing the shell game with three plastic medicine cups from her bedside table. Each time I told her to guess where the button was. When she didn't respond, I would pretend to be her and say, "I bet it's under there." Then I'd act surprised when it wasn't, and say,"Hmm, how did she do that?" Then I'd do it over again.

Now she was watching. I never quit talking, first being myself, then playing her part. Eventually, when I asked, "Now which one do you think it's under?" she pointed to one of the plastic cups. She was wrong.

I pretended I was her and said, "Now how did that lady do that?" I took the little girl's hands and said I would show her. Moving her hands, I showed her the trick to the shell game. As I moved the cup off the edge and let the button fall in her lap, I pretended I was perplexed and asked, "Now how did that little girl do that?"

She began to push the cups alone and I made certain to pick the wrong cup each time. This went on for about thirty minutes.

Then I said I'd rather do a puzzle. Clearing the table, I began to work on a jigsaw puzzle, handing her pieces and then pointing to where the piece would go. The entire time we sat, I was warring in the spirit and praying in my prayer language. To her, I probably just looked like a lady who was ready to sit there all day. The room became very quiet as she stared intently at the puzzle pieces in her hand. She seemed deep in thought. And then she spoke. "I killed my mother," she said.

This chapter is about being guided by God. How could any person have known what was stirring around in that little girl's heart? A psychiatrist might have worked with her for months or years and still not have been able to find out what was wrong. On a conscious level, she might not even have known what the problem was. But the problem was exposed with the guidance of God and the weapons He has left to us.

I won't go into all the details of the way God allowed me to minister to her. But I will say that it was so wonderful and exciting. I couldn't believe the words that came out of my mouth! The first words were, "Your mother's not dead." I explained to her how we all live forever somewhere and how her mother was with Jesus. I demonstrated taking off the body as I laid my coat aside.

By the time I was ready to leave, she had given her heart to Jesus and she was talking. She was so happy that one day she would be reunited with her mother in heaven. She had been left without hope and hope deferred makes the heart sick. The truth had brought hope.

This leads me to the final concept the Lord told me to teach children: the fact that there is an eternity and that we will spend it with Him in heaven.

GOD GUIDES THOSE WHO LISTEN

STUDY QUESTIONS FOR ADULTS (CHAPTER 9)

What is my responsibility in being able to hear God's voice?

Psalm 34:10 _____

Psalm 9:10 _____

Luke 11:9 _____

Prov. 8:17 _____

Matt. 6:33 _____

Will God always answer me?

Psalm 91:15 _____

John 10:3-4 _____

John 10:27 _____

John 18:37 _____

Rev. 3:20 _____

CHAPTER TEN

Children Need To Be Heavenly Minded

As you teach on the eternal, you will become more sensitive to the lost. Speaking of eternity lends itself to the subject of salvation.

My heart had been stirred to communicate the salvation message to the very young child in an effective way that would enable him to understand. Prayer on this specific subject led to the following lesson. Although originally intended for the very young child, this lesson has brought hundreds and hundreds of children, of all ages, to personally know and accept their Savior.

Activity — My Heart

(For this activity, you will need to copy the following drawings and then cut a large heart out of red paper. The size of the visual aids depends on how many children are watching as you present the lesson. For a small group, you can duplicate the pictures without enlarging them and use a construction paper heart. For a children's church setting, enlarge each to poster size and cut a large heart out of red poster board. Cut the drawings out and color them brightly.)

Do you know what this is, boys and girls? It's my heart. This is not my real heart. I made this one to show you what happens inside of a person's heart when they act in a certain way.

Our hearts are just like houses. They are like houses because feelings live in them. The place that we live in is called a house, so the place that our feelings live in is called a house, too. This is a story about a person who let some really bad feelings come live in her house and what happened as a result.

The first thing that she did was to let the feeling of fear come live in her heart. His name was Fearful Fred and he was afraid of many things. He made the little girl afraid, also. She was afraid that people wouldn't like her, no matter how nicely she treated them. I'm sorry to say she didn't treat them very nicely.

We don't need to be fearful or afraid if Jesus is in our hearts because He loves us even when we're not nice. In fact, He loves us no matter what we do. But He wants us to act nicely to people so we'll be happy.

This little girl, however, didn't know about Jesus. That's one of the reasons she let Fearful Fred come live in her house. Now Fearful Fred lived there so long that he started to feel as though he owned the place. He invited his friend, Bully Bill, to come and live in the heart with him.

With Bully Bill living in her heart, the little girl started pushing people around. The other kids didn't understand what she was feeling. They didn't know that when she pushed one of them off the swing set it was because she was afraid that if she asked them to play with her, they'd say no and reject her. They didn't see that it was the bad feelings making her act like a bully. The children all decided they didn't like playing with her. She lost all of her friends.

With no one to play with, the little girl grew very unhappy and bored. She just lay around the house all the time. Soon, another feeling came into her heart to live. This one was Slothful Sue. Slothful means lazy. And that's just what happened to the little girl. Because she didn't do anything, she became lazier and lazier.

So our little girl was becoming quite unhappy and miserable. I don't want to scare you by showing you all these ugly feelings. There really isn't someone called Fearful Fred or Bully Bill or Slothful Sue.

BULLY
BILL

FEARFUL
FRED

MAD MITCH

SLOTHFUL SUE

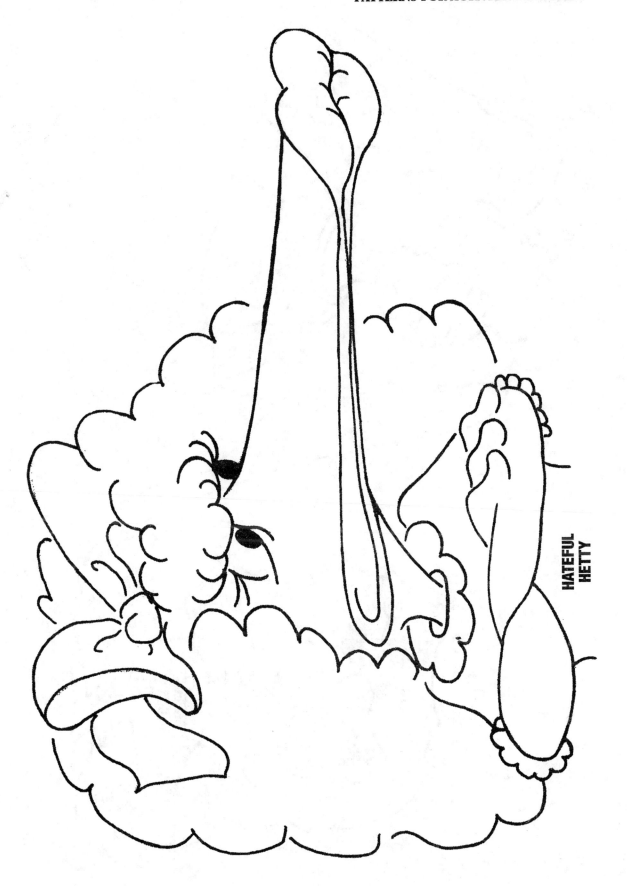

HATEFUL
HETTY

103

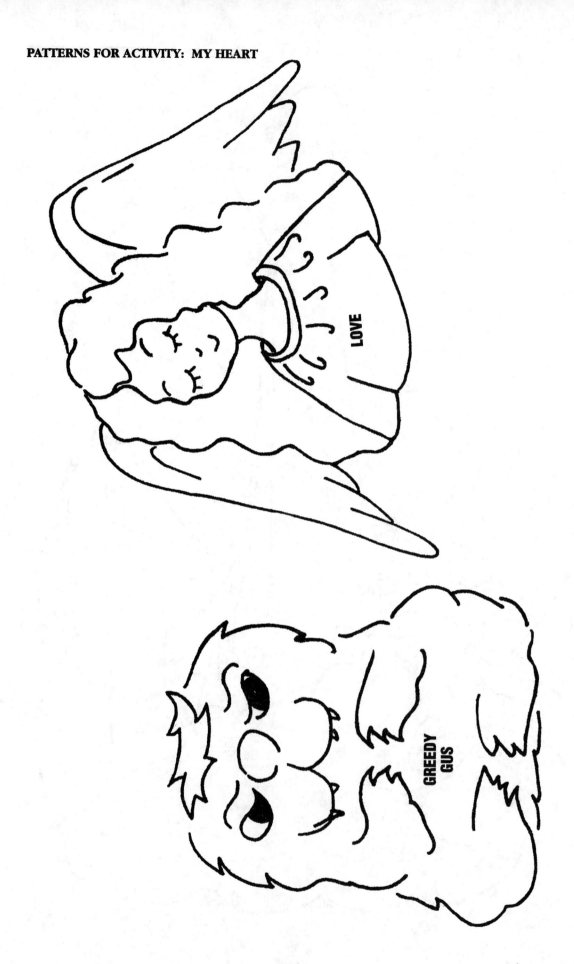

JOY

PEACE

This is just to show you what I think those feelings would look like if we could look into a person's heart. If we had the ability to look into the little girl's heart, we would say that this heart is a mess.

Here she was. She had Fearful Fred, Bully Bill and Slothful Sue. She didn't know what to do. She didn't know how to be any other way. Being bored and lazy all the time was a very unhappy state to be in. To escape these feelings, she would daydream about all the wonderful things she wished she had.

She already had one television set. But since she'd seen all its programs and reruns, she thought another TV might help. She had one bicycle. But now she started wanting a newer one. Pretty soon, she wanted everything. It didn't matter whether she needed it or not.

Oh, oh! Know what happened? Slothful Sue's cousin, Greedy Gus, had come to live in her heart, too. Now the little girl knew that she couldn't have all the things that she wanted, so this made her even more unhappy. Greed always causes much unhappiness, wherever he is. But again, even though the little girl had grown both unhappy and miserable, she just didn't know what to do about the situation.

One day at school, the teachers were giving away the leftovers from a bake sale. After all the children were finished with their lunches, they were allowed to go to the center table and have a cookie.

The little girl already had eaten her cookie, but she noticed that two cookies remained on the plate. She didn't care whether the other children had had their cookies or not. She wanted both of those cookies for herself. Just as her hand was about to reach the cookie plate, another child reached in and took one of the cookies.

As the other child walked away, nibbling the cookie that she had wanted, the greedy little girl thought, "I wanted them both. I am soooo mad! That makes me so mad I can't stand it!"

Oh, no! Not again! Do you know what happened this time? The little girl let Mad Mitch come to live in her heart.

Look at her heart. It is really starting to be a giant mess. It has filled up with all those nasty, horrible feelings. Only one thing happens when you get so many terrible feelings living together in one heart. They all get together and invite the meanest, nastiest feeling in the world in, mean old, nasty Hateful Hetty. This is the worst feeling anyone could ever have, because with hate living in your heart, you not only don't like anyone else, but you don't even like yourself.

By now, the little girl had become so unhappy she began to cry. Suddenly, she remembered something she had been taught in Sunday School. Jesus has the power to take away all the bad feelings you have in your heart. He is God's Son and He died for our sins. Our bad feelings are sins, so he can take them all away.

The little girl closed her eyes and prayed a prayer to Jesus. Do you know what she prayed? She said, "Jesus, I am so unhappy. Will You make me happy?"

Well, Jesus must already have been dealing with the little girl's heart, because she suddenly realized that she could never be happy as long as all those nasty feelings were living in her heart. So she asked Jesus to take away those nasty, sinful feelings from her heart and make her clean.

That's the most wonderful thing about Jesus. He always takes away nasty, sinful feelings. He doesn't want us to be unhappy. But we must ask Him.

Suddenly, the little girl wasn't fearful anymore. She didn't feel greedy or mad or slothful. All the hate was gone and she didn't want to push anyone around ever again. That's because Jesus had come to live in her heart. Jesus isn't afraid of anyone so the little girl wasn't afraid. Jesus isn't greedy, mad or slothful. He doesn't hate anyone, either. Jesus loves everyone. Jesus really cleaned up her heart.

Do you know what else? Jesus didn't just clean up her heart and leave it empty. He sent His love to live in her heart. With all that love in her, she started making friends. If you have love in your heart, do you push people off swing sets? No! You give your swing away.

So the children started to like her because she was treating them nicely. Love treats people kindly and considerately. She made so many friends that Love invited its friend, Joy, to come and live in her heart, also. With so much Love and Joy in her heart, she just went around singing all the time and all the people started to really like to be around her. Love and Joy began to feel so much at home in her heart that they invited their cousin, Peace, to come and live with them, also.

Now look at the little girl's heart. Isn't it beautiful? Isn't it much nicer to have all those wonderful feelings in there instead of all those ugly, nasty ones? Which heart would you rather have?

Maybe some of you right now have nasty feelings in your heart. Maybe you even have some we didn't show you here today. How many of you would like Jesus to come right now into your heart and take away any nasty feelings or sins that are in there? He will come and clean you up and fill you with wonderful feelings. (Pray sinner's prayer here.)

Duplicating the pictures without enlarging them, the kids colored and cut them out and put them in a construction paper folder marked "Witnessing Kit." Sharing this little story with relatives and friends, they led 28 people to Jesus in a two-week period.

ETERNITY

When I was a young girl in a Baptist church, an evangelist came to town. He told a story I have never forgotten: "Pretend this world is ten times bigger than it really is. Pretend that it is made of solid steel. Now every hundred years or so, a little white dove flies by and softly brushes the tip of his wing against that steel ball. By the time that steel ball has been worn down to the size of a BB, not one-half of a second will have passed in eternity."

That story made this life seem to have little significance. It gave me a much larger view of eternity. (At that time, I had a father who was an alcoholic and no solid biblical teaching on how to use my faith. Many times I could have been swallowed up in despair if I had not known that this earth is not my home.)

This story really impresses on the children how long eternity must be, especially if you have brushed each of their faces with the soft feather from the Christmas dove. It would be good to give each of them their own BB to handle and take home. Each time I teach on eternity I review this story.

I worked diligently, when my children were little, to give them a view of the eternal. As preschoolers, this was done very simplistically, at a level that they could comprehend.

"Oh, I saw you share your toy with that little girl. Do you know what just happened?" I would ask. "Jesus just dropped a toy in your toy box in heaven."

The children really enjoyed building up treasures in heaven, often running in, out of breath, to tell me of some good deed that they had just done that would increase their stockpile of toys in heaven. If this offends you, it shouldn't, because God says in His Word that there are rewards for those who serve Him.

"But without faith it is impossible to please him; for he that cometh to God must believe that he is, and that he is a rewarder of them that diligently seek him."

Hebrews 11:6

"And, behold, I come quickly; and my reward is with me, to give every man according as his work shall be."

Revelations 22:12

"But love ye your enemies, and do good, and lend, hoping for nothing again; and your reward shall be great, and ye shall be the children of the Highest: for he is kind unto the unthankful and to the evil."

Luke 6:35

"Rejoice ye in that day, and leap for joy: for behold, your reward is great in heaven."

Luke 6:23

As the children grew older, we referred to "jewels" in our heavenly treasure chest. One day, we were driving down the road in a hurry to reach the mall before a certain store closed. There was an old Spanish lady, walking at the side of the road, carrying a grocery bag. I pulled over to offer her a ride. The children in unison, wailed, "Oh, don't stop. You're gonna make us late. She won't ride with a stranger anyway."

She happily accepted our ride, pointing directions to her home, because there was a language barrier between us. It was only a five-minute drive, but would have been a hefty walk for the elderly lady carrying her heavy bag. This woman kept thanking us over and over again in Spanish and I could see from my children's faces, they'd had a change of heart.

As soon as she was out of the car and I had pulled away, I excitedly asked, "Did you see who that was? Did you recognize who was just in our car?" A puzzled look came over all their faces. They were certain they'd never seen her before.

"Why, that was Jesus," I told them. "That was Jesus, walking down the road disguised as an old Spanish lady. We just helped Him. Jesus just dropped a jewel in our heavenly treasure chest and no one can ever take it from us. That reward will be waiting for us when we get to heaven."

111

My youngest acted very disbelieving and said, "She didn't look anything like Jesus to me."

I told them that in His Word, God promises that whatever we do to anyone, we've done to Him. Finally, they were convinced.

And when we arrived at the mall, the store was open for an extra hour because of a special sale.

"And these words, which I command thee this day, shall be in thine heart: And thou shalt teach them diligently unto thy children, and shalt talk of them when thou sittest in thine house, and when thou walkest by the way, and when thou liest down, and when thou risest up."

Deuteronomy 6:6,7

I was walking by the way, teaching them His Word. In this instance, the Word was from Matthew:

"Inasmuch as ye have done it unto one of the least of these my brethren, ye have done it unto me."

Matthew 25:40

"Lay not up for yourselves treasures upon earth, where moth and rust doth corrupt, and where thieves break through and steal: But lay up for yourselves treasures in heaven, where neither moth nor rust doth corrupt, and where thieves do not break through and steal: For where your treasure is, there will your heart be also.

Matthew 6:19-21

A parent has far greater opportunity to teach their children than you do. The little time you have with them in the class is probably the only time you'll have with them each week. Take advantage of that time. Bring in as many of your outside experiences as you can. We acted out the story of the old Spanish woman, using four chairs as car seats. We even dropped a jewel into a treasure chest.

Activity — You Can't Take It With You

Take a doll and hold it over a table filled with all kinds of stuff — toys, jewelry, letters from friends, etc. Start on one side of the table, a foot or so away from the edge, holding the doll in the air. Explain that this is what they were like before they were born. They had no clothes, toys or anything else. Then they entered this world. As the doll passes over the table, hold it in your arms in such a way that you can begin piling the things from the table on top of it.

Explain to the children that the table represents our world and all the things they can accumulate from it while passing through. When the doll reaches the other side of the table, explain that all the stuff must be left here in the world and that as the doll leaves, it has exactly what it had when it entered the world.

"For we brought nothing into this world, and it is certain we can carry nothing out."

I Timothy 6:7

As the old song goes, "Only one life; t'will soon be passed, only what's done for Christ will last." Your goal is to get the children to focus on the lasting, the eternal.

Activity — Treasures in Heaven

One way to do this would be to put two boxes on a table. One is marked temporary, one is marked eternal. Make up situations that would bring a temporary reward. I take my money and buy ice cream. Drop an item into the temporary reward. I enjoyed the taste and had fun eating it. Now pretend we take our money and give it in an offering that goes to missions. The item goes into the eternal box.

When our life here on earth comes to an end, the box that says eternal will be waiting for us with Jesus. The box that says temporary cannot go along. It goes in the garbage can. So why do we labor for the temporary?

For many years, we all lived for the "pie in the sky" in the "sweet by and by," as they say. The devil beat us up here on earth.

Solid biblical teaching came along and showed us that the devil is under our feet and that we don't have to wait to be blessed and happy. Glory! But let's not trade away our blessed hope to walk in victory now. We can have it all. We can be blessed coming in and blessed going out.

The twenty-first chapter of Revelation gives a vivid description of heaven. Use as many visuals as possible to illustrate this for the children. You might take in a pearl ring and explain how costly it is. You could show them a colored advertisement for jewelry. Tell them how big one of the twelve gates of heaven is, and explain that each gate is made from a single pearl. Then try to compute the cost of a single gate. Have the children try to imagine how high a stack of money they would need to buy just one of the gates in heaven. Compare that to the price of a gate on an earthly mansion. Showing them how much bigger and better and magnificent heaven is over anything we've ever dreamed of here. What you are actually doing is teaching them how to meditate the Word, to not just hear, but to hear with understanding, to comprehend what is being said.

Do everything you can to help them grasp the reality of streets of gold and foundations of jewels. Stress over and over and over again that the words in the Bible are true.

Finally, the most wonderful thing about heaven is that God Himself will be there with us. We want to move the children through the important step of what God has, to the all important step of who God is. This brings us back full circle — to our Designer.

My Father Is Preparing A House For Me

STUDY QUESTIONS FOR ADULTS (CHAPTER 10)

How do I know God wants me to be with Him in heaven?

John 17:23 _____

Rev. 21:3 _____

How do I know what heaven will be like?

Rev. 21:1-4 _____

Rev. 21:10-27 _____

Rev. 22:1-5 _____

Heb. 11:16 _____

Rev. 22:17 _____

How can I be certain I'm going there?

Eph. 2:8,9 _____

John 6:47 _____

John 14:1-3 _____

About the Author

CHARLOTTE RAHRIG has attended Rhema Bible Training Center and is an AFCM-ordained Children's Pastor who ministers to children in both churches and schools. She has taught at South Florida Bible Training Center and at Charismalife International Children's Ministry Conferences as a workshop leader. Charlotte has also held seminars overseas. She has published books in the U.S., Russia, and South America.

Charlotte is currently on radio daily with a devotional for children and is on the Internet worldwide. She has appeared on the "700 Club," the Trinity Broadcasting Network, and with James Kennedy. She has also been a guest on "Point of View," a national radio show hosted by Marlin Maddoux.

Charlotte's home church is Believer's Victory Church in West Palm Beach, Florida.

Her vision is to be instrumental in ushering in the end time revival among children with the motto:

"PREACH THE BLOOD • WIN SOULS• KNOW GOD"

For information on seminars, write:

Charlotte Rahrig

P.O. Box 700565, Tulsa, Oklahoma 74170

Additional copies of this book are available from your local bookstore.

Harrison House
Tulsa, Oklahoma 74153